There's Always Room at the Table

There's Always Room *at the* Table

Farmhouse Recipes
from My Family to Yours

Kaleb Wyse

HARVEST
An Imprint of WILLIAM MORROW

The recipes in this book are for you,

so that you will feel excited and ready to experience simple home food. This is for the home cook who quietly puts food on the table daily. I owe my know-how and blind confidence to those quiet cooks. Mom, my grandmas, and the generations before who didn't see kitchen work as relentless but as a way to nourish and grow their families.

Contents

Introduction

We all have our own stories when it comes to food. And it makes sense: our days are often centered around food. What we're eating, when we're going to eat, and who we're sharing that meal with are commonplace thoughts for many. I hope I'm not the only one who wakes up wondering what they're going to cook for dinner! Food memories, like all memories, can be a wild ride: some scrumptious and some not so delicious.

For me, it's all about the round oak table in the center of my childhood kitchen, and my mom, dad, sister, and me all sharing a homemade meal together. We were a tight-knit family who enjoyed our time gathered at that table, except for the occasional tear when my sister had to endure a meal she couldn't stand. But one thing was a constant: good food. Most of it was homemade, though my mom will occasionally remind me that Hamburger Helper did make a guest appearance every now and then.

No, it wasn't heaven, just a small family farm in southeast Iowa. You know the line from a popular baseball movie, "Is this heaven? No, it's Iowa"? That's my sentiment when I reflect on my youth. There were fields stretching as far as the eye could see, with rows and rows of corn and soybeans that seemed to begin with the sunrise in the morning and end with the sunset at night.

My childhood took place in the same house where my great-grandparents raised their family, a house that would become a sanctuary for future generations. After my grandparents raised their children, my parents moved back in, extending the tradition. Sounds a bit too idyllic, right? Well, it kinda was, but this was the picture of life for my family's existence on the farm. My dad was a farmer practically from birth, learning to walk and beginning to work the land at almost the same time. He truly loved what he did and felt he was the luckiest guy being able to farm for a living. Mom, on the other hand, had her own well-matched strengths both in the kitchen and garden, growing green beans, peas, tomatoes, greens, peppers, squash, and strawberries. You name it, and she pretty much grew it.

And let's not forget my grandmas; they were frequently at our home, always helping out in the garden or house, especially during the summer preserving frenzy. Back then, if you wanted a large variety of fresh produce in Iowa and high-quality frozen goods for winter, you had to grow it. Plus, we needed to save whatever money we could, so growing and preserving food was Mom's way of chipping in on the farm. The farm really was a labor of love and necessity for everyone involved.

Fast-forward to my days in high school, and I began to realize I wouldn't be quite the same farmer as my dad. Farming the fields my family has cultivated for generations was not what I ever saw for myself. I love the farm and land, but I always knew I'd have a different path, and I think Dad knew that, too. He passed away from pancreatic cancer while I was a junior in high school, but Mom stayed on the farm, carrying on the traditions she knew and loved. I went off to college in Virginia, and while I loved the change of scenery (those mountains!), I always knew I'd come back to Iowa. Today, most farm-raised kids don't boomerang back home after college. I'll consider myself an anomaly, choosing to settle not in the city but in my grandparents' house right across the road from my childhood home. Growing up, I always felt a strong connection to the fact that I'd be the fourth generation to have the chance to live on our farm. After Dad passed away, that feeling grew stronger, becoming a compelling need. Moving home was a blend of nostalgia and loss: Dad's absence on the farm each day, juxtaposed with the proximity to the thing he loved so dearly. He *was* the farm, and his whole being was intertwined into every field he plowed each spring. At the time, moving home was how I knew I'd still feel his presence and like a piece of Dad was ever-present.

After moving back home, I began working as an accountant, which is what I studied for in college, but it was no surprise that I was utterly unhappy. People's faces were priceless when they heard me say that I was an accountant. Like, "You, really?" I get it, though. Anyone who knew me also knew I was not one to sit at a desk or in an office. I was constantly moving, adding flower gardens in junior high, working in a camp kitchen in high school, and redoing the house in my free time. Accounting was never on my radar until I needed to declare a major in college. I should note that accounting is a great field, and I know people who love it. But this simply was not what I was meant to do. I loved my house and living where I grew up, but I didn't love my work.

So, to keep myself sane, I started a vegetable garden in my backyard. Even though Mom had a huge garden right across the road, I craved a garden to call my own. I worked until dark every night, harvesting produce, preserving jars of produce to store in my basement, putting in new flower beds, and joyfully making mistakes all along the way. Turns out, it became more than just a garden; it was my happy space, an outlet for my creativity to grow.

Eventually, I decided to create a website and social media handles to share everything I held close to my heart. The problem was, I initially hesitated to share my Iowa food stories. It felt a bit awkward to talk about everything I

cherished. What could a guy from Iowa possibly add to the culinary chatter, especially when there's so much "new" in the food scene? I had this lingering idea, probably fueled by Mom, both grandmas, and what I perceived as the Midwest stereotype, that our homegrown meals were nothing out of the ordinary. Even Grandma Alice, when praised with a compliment after a delicious meal, insists, "Oh, it's nothing special. Just the normal food I make." So, for the longest time, I viewed our food as something too ordinary to share: a misconception I held onto until 2020 hit, and we were all stuck at home. Suddenly, the food I grew up on became the comforting dose of nostalgia we all craved.

So, I began sharing my garden adventures along with the food I know. It was like flipping on a light switch. People got it. They connected with my roots and the food I was making. It turns out, the things I thought were too regular were hitting the sweet spot of nostalgia for some, and were a breath of fresh air for others. And that's the magic of food, right? It has this incredible power to unite us and resurrect memories. One bite can transport us to a cozy holiday gathering at Grandma's table, or the scent wafting from a beloved recipe baking in the oven can whisk us back to those cherished moments in Mom's kitchen.

This cookbook is a living scrapbook of my family through the generations. The recipes aren't set in stone; they live and breathe just like us. Ingredients change, tastes evolve, but the base flavors stay true. These recipes, at their core, are a shout-out to the amazing women in my family who juggled everything: gardening, preserving, and making every single meal.

In a world where home-cooked meals are becoming a super-rare sighting, this cookbook is my way of saying, "Well, hello, old friend." Each recipe has a story from my life or my family's past, but trust me, none of them are outdated. Just like with people, with recipes there's always room at the table. This is my invitation for you to enjoy the timeless joy of shared meals, creating the moments you can savor.

HWS

Jodi Wyse

Who's in This Story

When I talk about my family and how
they've shaped me, I worry I'll sound
cliché. We all are shaped by family. For
better or worse, they're a part of who we
become, but they don't write the entire
story. Throughout this book, I'll mention
and reference many family members, so
I think introducing each of them here is
a good idea. Think of this as a succinct
bio that helps set the stage for who these
people are (or were) and how they're a
part of my life.

Dad
Curt (whose full
name was Curtis, but
I never heard anyone
call him that)

My dad was a quiet giant, standing at about 6 foot 4 and very slender. He had a good sense of humor, but not everyone had the privilege to know that. Dad was never loud or overly extroverted, so too many people thought of him as standoffish, but he was exactly the opposite. He knew when to use the right words and when to let silence do the talking. Dad passed away in 2004 from pancreatic cancer after a short six-month battle. As it does for so many, this marked a new chapter in our family and left a hole we'd certainly all feel for life. Dad was the farm. He adored what he did and felt his purpose was to farm our land. That's probably why I ended up seeking out a "job" that was also my passion. Without Dad, I may never have experienced seeing someone so content and in love with life. I kid you not; every family vacation, Dad couldn't wait to get home and see the farm. As soon as it was in view, he'd say, "Who lives there? They must be pretty lucky."

Mom
Jodi or Jodi Sue

Sometimes, I like using her first and middle names because I find it fun to call her Jodi Sue; it rolls off the tongue nicely. My mom is hands down the most caring and tender-hearted person I know. She's got this deep love that drives her to work tirelessly and selflessly for anyone in the family. When it's warm or kinda warm (hey, this is Iowa, and a 45°F day in late winter feels like a heatwave), you can bet Mom's soaking up the outdoors. Her garden, a mix of vegetables and flowers, always looks picture-perfect. In cooler months, Mom sews. I can still recall hearing the hum of her Bernina sewing machine as she'd work on mending for others or crafting clothing for herself. Mom taught me everything without teaching me anything. She let me watch, follow, and eventually cook, bake, preserve, and garden as I pleased. After Dad passed away, in 2010 Mom remarried Allan, who had lost his wife to cancer. Together, they continue to live across the road in the "homeplace" where I grew up.

Kelsey
My sister

There were two of us growing up, and we were super close, other than the occasional fight. Do you remember the Buddy doll commercial from the '90s with that ridiculously catchy jingle?

We'd strut around the farm arm in arm, belting out that tune like it was our jam. Kelsey claims she's slightly quieter and more reserved than I am, and I can't help but see a hefty dose of Dad in her. She knows when to use the words needed in just the right way. Kelsey's a determined worker who never seems to stop. Her house is always spotless, her kids are always well-fed, and she's a Realtor on top of all that. She now lives in Virginia with her husband, Kendal, along with my nieces, Kaidence and Karcyn, and my nephew, Kyan. But Mom and I will never stop trying to get them all to move back to Iowa. I'll keep you posted on how that goes!

Grandma Conrad
Joyce, my mom's mom

Grandma Conrad is where Mom's kind heart comes from. Joyce grew up and lived on her farm, a mere five miles from where I grew up. Actually, most of the family lived within this cozy five-mile radius. Grandma Conrad was a force, tirelessly tending to her flawless yard and garden. She often went to her mom's house (Great-Grandma Hirschy) to help her in any way she could. Storytime with Grandma Conrad was the best, as she always had a tale or a witty remark up her sleeve. One classic was her "COD curve" routine. Whenever you'd be in the backseat of a car with her and go around a tight curve, forcing you to bump shoulders, she'd say that was a COD curve. Playing along, I'd ask what a COD curve was. That twinkle in her eye would appear, she'd smirk, and drop the punchline: "Come Over, Dear." Cue her chuckles. Joyce was a master seamstress, canner, baker, and cook, you name it. When her husband, Edwin, passed away when she was forty-four (similar to Mom's story with Dad), she lost a bit of the fire for cooking and baking but never for preserving. The instant you walked into her house, you would smell mustard pickles and peppernuts. My knack for tweaking recipes actually comes straight from Grandma Conrad. She'd have something on the counter, insist I taste it, and then dive in with my critique. Honestly, most times, the adjustments she made were subtle: a pinch less salt, a tad less sugar. Back then, I thought it was trivial, but looking at her recipes now, with all those dated adjustments, I totally get it. Getting that recipe just right was her mission, and she did it well.

Grandma Alice
My dad's mom

Growing up, Grandma Alice and Grandpa Gene were practically neighbors, living right across the road. And let me tell you, Grandma redefines the word "work." The concept of relaxing is foreign to her because she thrives on staying busy. She grew up on a farm, helping her dad with chores. After marrying Grandpa Gene, she moved to my childhood farm and jumped right in, helping with chores, fieldwork, hauling grain during harvest, tending to a massive garden, preserving food, volunteering at church, and, to top it off, quilting. All of this while raising two kids, one of them being my dad. When Mom and Dad first got married, they actually lived across the road from where Dad grew up. Then, when my parents took over the farm, they swapped houses with Grandpa and Grandma. Now, I'm living in the same house that holds some of my idyllic memories of going to Grandma's. She'd bake cookies with us, teach Kelsey and me the art of cross-stitch, and somehow make cleaning feel like it was fun. How did she do that? Fast-forward to today, and I'm very lucky to have her just five miles away in town. She still whips up food when the family gathers, but good luck trying to get her to accept any help when it comes to the meal. She might just be the hardest worker I know.

Grandpa Gene
My dad's dad (we simply call him Grandpa since we only knew one grandpa)

Grandpa is a true gentle giant, not because he's tall or overly large, but because his kindness and quiet generosity have a way of filling up any room. In 1964, he purchased the farm from his parents, who weren't exactly thrilled about farming, having weathered the Great Depression. But Grandpa powered through and put in the hard work. Over the years, Grandpa, who'll make sure to say he couldn't have done it without Grandma, expanded the farm. He and my dad were best friends and worked together on the farm each day. I can still recall the sweet sound of Grandpa's four-wheeler revving up in the early morning as he made his way to our place, ready for a full day of work with Dad. Even though he lives in town now, Grandpa still enjoys a drive past the fields to see how the crops are growing, just like a true farmer.

Great-Grandma Hirschy
Lydia, my mom's maternal grandma

Although I never had the chance to know Great-Grandma Hirschy personally, it feels like I do through the vivid stories shared by Mom and Grandma Conrad. And there's a common theme through all three generations: a love for a bountiful garden and vibrant flowers. Times were tough when Lydia was raising her family, with no room for frivolous things, so she took matters into her own hands, creating things to bring joy to her family instead. I've heard countless stories through the years about her cheese hanging in the basement, the butter she churned, the cookies she baked, and the legendary homemade tomato soup topped with potato chips that she'd serve my mom after school. Trust me, if you haven't tried that combo, you're missing out and need to immediately. Actually, bookmark this page, go try it, and return when you're finished eating. To give you a glimpse of the size of her garden, she once noted in her diary about the day her kids helped to pick strawberries. After collecting a whopping 199 pints of fresh berries, her son-in-law insisted there must be one more. After a bit more searching, they hit the evenly numbered 200 pints. And mind you, that was just one item from her garden. Imagine the incredible amount of work she put in during her life.

Great-Grandma Frances
My dad's paternal grandma

Frances would get up at the crack of dawn, milk the cows, and then make breakfast for her family, all before 8 a.m. And that was just the warm-up. The rest of her day was a whirlwind of chicken-tending, chores, gardening, preserving food, and raising her four kids. Even after she moved off the family farm, she couldn't resist raising chickens on the property because, according to her, there was no store-bought bird that could compare. My memories of Great-Grandma recall her as a quiet, sweet old woman who'd keep an eye on me when Mom was grocery shopping. The image of her, wearing oversized prescription sunglasses, peering over the steering wheel of her massive Lincoln to treat me to ice cream, is etched in my mind. Little did I know, she had a vibrant and active life long before I came into the picture. She meticulously documented every vacation and major life event in extensive scrapbooks. I love the story of their family road trip to Oregon, quite a decent distance from Iowa. She packed the car with jars of home-preserved foods, and on their way, they'd scout out hotels with kitchens or stop at roadside campsites to cook. That's a level of dedication to preserving and canning that blows my mind, and I can't imagine anyone doing the same today. I'm so thankful she passed down at least a bit of her knowledge to me.

Each of these incredible individuals has left an indelible mark on my life. Even if I didn't have the chance to meet or know some of them intimately, their influence echoes through the family they raised. The nurturing spirit, the love for food, and the joy of growing a garden—all of these traits have been passed down from each one of them. I'm grateful to have shared a glimpse of their stories with you, connecting our lives through the rich picture of family history.

About This Book

In putting together this cookbook,
I had three simple rules for picking the
recipes:

1. The dishes had to be reminiscent of
   those prepared by my mom, grandmas,
   or even great-grandmas.

2. The ingredients had to be readily
   available in my southeastern Iowa
   grocery stores, meaning that they'd be
   available for pretty much anyone else.

3. The resulting recipes had to be both
   no-nonsense and delicious.

You might notice I didn't throw in words such as "quick" or "fast." Not all food should be made in a rush. Sure, some recipes in this book can be your go-to for a speedy meal, but others require some time. Take, for example, Great-Grandma Hirschy's Donuts (page 8). They need time to rise and be fried, but trust me, they're worth the wait. We all love shortcuts, like those recipes for air-fryer donuts, but sometimes, putting in the extra effort is what makes the calories totally worth it. The flavor in each step of making those donuts is what sets them apart.

Unlike the generations that worked in my kitchen before me, I've got some ingredients in my pantry that they couldn't even dream up. I still stock up on jars of home-preserved goods like tomatoes, salsa, green beans, peppers, pears, peaches, and pickles. But I've tweaked these recipes to fit things you can buy at the store.

Don't let any recipe stress you out. Case in point: the homemade noodles recipe (see Great-Grandma Hirschy's Egg Noodles, page 133). Making noodles might sound like a whole project, but it's surprisingly easy and a great way to learn the basics. Yeah, you can grab noodles off the shelf, but there's something about fresh noodles that's way better than the store-bought ones that have been sitting on the shelf forever. We've all found that forgotten box of noodles in the back of the pantry, right?

Some recipes might sound weird if you're not from Iowa or the Midwest. For instance, take the pork tenderloin sandwich (page 43). This is an Iowa original that every Iowan will have a memory of. The pork loin is pounded thin, breaded, and fried. Restaurants in Iowa will even gain notoriety for having a tenderloin the size of a dinner plate while still using a small hamburger bun. I get it: foods can vary across the United States, but be brave and give everything a shot. A bunch of these unique recipes came to life because we needed to get creative with leftovers. And trust me, they turned out to be delicious surprises.

I don't look at any recipe as outdated. Food trends come and go, but good food and the memories it creates endures. Some of these recipes are from my '90s childhood on the farm. We had our fair share of convenience foods, such as Hamburger Helper night during mom's sewing classes. There are no boxed items in this book, though. But you'll find my spin on childhood classics like seven-layer dip (see Layered Bean Dip, page 145) or a fresh take on broccoli and cauliflower salad (see Roasted Broccoli & Cauliflower Salad, page 135).

With that said, get in the kitchen, start cooking, and make sure to enjoy yourself!

Pantry Staples

One of the golden rules for this cookbook is that all ingredients should be easy to find, with nothing too out of the ordinary. If it's on the shelves in my rural part of southeastern Iowa, it's safe to assume you'll be able to find it, too, wherever you live.

My pantry today doesn't exactly mirror what the previous generations on my farm had in theirs. Things slowly and surely evolve; even here in Iowa, we're getting our hands on more and more grocery items that were previously reserved for bigger cities. That said, there are a few ingredients in this book that may be new to some. So, if it's an ingredient my mom has ever asked me about, then I figured it's a good idea to explain it here.

Kosher salt will always be the salt of choice listed in my recipes, and it's become a standard in many kitchens. The grains of kosher salt are slightly larger and flakier than regular iodized salt, and it has no added ingredients or anticaking agents. It's important to note that you can use any salt you have on hand, but the amount must be adjusted as kosher salt measures differently than table salt. As a general rule, if you only have table salt, use approximately half the amount listed for kosher salt. All of my recipes use Diamond Crystal kosher salt. If you use a different brand of kosher salt, the amount will need to be adjusted accordingly.

Dijon mustard is my go-to for both a creamy vinaigrette and as a way to add a secret flavor boost to pretty much anything. Tangy, savory, and sharp, it brings a lot to the table. The mustard emulsifies oil and vinegar for a balanced dressing, and it can add a slight kick to a meal, like in my Biscuit Egg Quiche (page 11). Talk about versatility! Dijon is a magical ingredient that enhances flavor just like an amazing seasoning.

Tahini is a ground paste made from sesame seeds and is widely available at any grocery store. It's traditionally used as an ingredient in hummus, but its potential extends far beyond that. I personally love to use tahini in dips, substituting it for nut butter to add a savory touch to a recipe, and in this cookbook, it's used in my favorite Caesar dressing (see Tahini Caesar Dressing, page 109). If you haven't given tahini a spot in your pantry yet, consider buying a jar during your next grocery run. You may just discover a new favorite ingredient with countless possibilities.

Unsalted butter is a staple ingredient across all recipes in this cookbook. When I initially began developing recipes, I didn't distinguish between unsalted and salted butter, often using whichever was available. It was a casual approach, and I assumed others would do the same. While butter is butter, the issue lies in the salt content of salted butter, which varies between brands. To maintain consistent salt levels and ensure you savor each recipe as intended, I recommend using unsalted butter and sticking to the specified amount. But, if salted butter is the only thing in your refrigerator, just know that you may need to adjust the listed salt amount accordingly.

Yeast is a pantry staple for me, always stocked in generous amounts stored in an airtight jar in the freezer, which is the secret to keeping it fresh for a long time. Every recipe in this cookbook using yeast calls for instant yeast (sometimes labeled fast-acting or quick-rise), and that's for two main reasons: first, instant yeast, with its smaller granules, skips the warm water dissolving time, making the recipe easier and slashing the overall recipe time. Simply add it right to the flour. Second, instant yeast can endure higher temperatures without killing the rising power. You can grab instant yeast in bulk or in individual packages, so when you see 2¼ teaspoons called for in a recipe, that's the classic amount found in one yeast package.

Whole milk is listed on every recipe instead of the more generic word "milk." So it begs the question: will fat-free, 1%, or 2% milk also work? The answer is yes, and I've experimented with milk with varying fat levels when baking and cooking. Whole milk is suggested because it will give you the most flavor in your recipe. Why is that? It's all about fat content. Whole milk has more milk fat, and we all know that fat equals flavor. The fat difference in the overall recipe is nominal compared to the added flavor the whole milk provides. It's totally worth it!

Garlic may very well take the spotlight in this cookbook, and that's because I just can't get enough of it! Years ago, my garlic world revolved around garlic powder or garlic salt, both solid choices for that extra oomph in a recipe. But let me tell you, they can't compete with what real garlic can add to a dish. While I still use garlic powder in my party mix, nothing beats the bold flavor of fresh garlic. My garden beds are filled with garlic because it's such an easy plant to grow. Simply plant individual cloves in the ground in the fall, and come June, beautiful garlic bulbs will be ready.

Fresh herbs are one of the most important things in my refrigerator. This is a big difference from my mom's refrigerator while I was growing up: there was nary a fresh herb to be found. Back then, grocery stores weren't stocking the herb aisle quite like they do now, and even with a massive garden, we weren't swimming in herbs like I am these days. The recipes in this cookbook that use fresh herbs are built intentionally with the flavor and texture that only fresh herbs can add. But you'll also find that I have recipes using dried herbs. I chose fresh or dried for a specific reason, so there isn't usually an easy swap between the two.

Breakfast

The first meal of the day usually turns into a quick routine born of sheer necessity. Most days call for something speedy to fuel up before leaving for school or work. These recipes aren't here to disrupt your early morning weekday hustle but instead shake things up when you crave a break from the usual. Some of these recipes are quick and easy, like my Dad's Cheesy Eggs (page 25), and then there are the ones that need a bit of prep and foresight, like the Overnight French Toast Stick Casserole (page 3). Don't be afraid to ditch the morning rush and sit down with your breakfast to savor something different. Get ready for a tasty detour from the ordinary.

Overnight French Toast Stick Casserole

— **Serves 8** —

I grew up during the '90s, when frozen breakfast foods were super popular. While I was lucky to have a mom who would make most meals from scratch, that didn't mean my sister, Kelsey, and I refrained from asking for the grocery store foods that were all the rage. One of our favorites was French toast sticks. Mom wouldn't buy them often, but it felt like Christmas Day when she did. Before school, we'd pop them in the toaster and, within minutes, have a maple syrup–drenched breakfast. I've tried the same store-bought French toast sticks in the intervening years and am shocked at their lack of flavor. They're only sweet with not much else to offer. This recipe is what a French toast stick should be, in my opinion, with two key swaps from the grocery store version. The first is good bread, which makes all the difference. When possible, choose an enriched bread, like brioche. The egg and butter in a brioche loaf will add to the richness of the French toast. The second is a good custard mixture. The correct ratio of eggs, milk, and cream will create a rich, bready interior with a crisp, buttery exterior. Think of these as an adult French toast stick that will also satisfy any kid.

1 loaf bread, preferably brioche, cut into slices ½ inch thick
7 large eggs
1¾ cups whole milk
1 cup heavy cream
1 teaspoon vanilla extract
2 teaspoons grated orange zest
¾ cup plus 2 tablespoons granulated sugar
½ teaspoon kosher salt
2 teaspoons ground cinnamon
Nonstick baking spray
Powdered sugar
Maple syrup

With the bottom of each slice of bread facing you, cut vertically into 4 equal sticks and set them aside.

In a large bowl, whisk the eggs until smooth. Add the milk, heavy cream, vanilla, orange zest, ¾ cup of the granulated sugar, the salt, and 1 teaspoon of the cinnamon. Whisk to combine.

Grease a 9 × 13-inch baking dish. Arrange the sticks of bread in rows, overlapping slightly. Slowly pour the custard mixture over the pieces, making sure to soak each piece. Cover and refrigerate overnight (about 8 hours).

When ready to bake, preheat the oven to 350°F.

In a small bowl, combine the remaining 2 tablespoons granulated sugar and remaining 1 teaspoon cinnamon. Sprinkle the mixture over the French toast sticks.

Bake until the French toast is puffed and browned, 45 to 55 minutes.

Serve with a dusting of powdered sugar and maple syrup.

Cinnamon Rolls with Brown Butter Frosting

— Makes 12 rolls —

Grandma Conrad made the best cinnamon rolls. They were light, fluffy, and melt-in-your-mouth perfection. In high school I started to pay attention to how Grandma made her rolls. I would spend hours with her, watching her make them and asking questions along the way. The rolls always seemed straightforward, but I could never seem to get them just right. Unlike Grandma's, mine would often be coarse and dry. Over time I found a slightly enriched dough was best. Grandma loved to work with a recipe until it was precisely the way she wanted it, so I know she would approve of my take on her cinnamon rolls, a slightly enriched dough that I've worked on for years to perfect. In this recipe, the dough is easy and forgiving with a fluffy, rich texture. Enriching the dough with butter makes it more elastic and easier to work with, and the perfect amount of flour ensures that the rolls will not turn out dry. The brown butter frosting, which Grandma always used, helps add a caramel-like nuttiness to the rolls that finishes them perfectly—some things never change.

FOR THE ROLLS

1 cup whole milk, warmed to 100° to 110°F
4 tablespoons unsalted butter, at room
    temperature
¾ teaspoon kosher salt
½ cup granulated sugar
1 large egg, beaten
4 cups all-purpose flour
2¼ teaspoons (1 envelope) instant yeast
Softened butter, for the baking dish
½ cup packed light brown sugar
1 tablespoon ground cinnamon
4 tablespoons unsalted butter, melted

FOR THE ICING

4 tablespoons unsalted butter
1½ teaspoons vanilla extract
¼ cup heavy cream
¼ teaspoon kosher salt
2 cups powdered sugar, sifted

Make the rolls: In a stand mixer fitted with the dough hook, combine the warm milk, room-temperature butter, salt, granulated sugar, egg, flour, and instant yeast. Mix the dough on medium-low speed until it is shaggy, 2 to 3 minutes. Turn the mixer to medium speed and continue kneading the dough until it becomes cohesive and starts pulling away from the sides of the bowl, 5 to 6 minutes.

Finish kneading the dough by hand on a lightly floured surface. Knead the dough until it is smooth and easily releases from the counter while kneading. It should feel slightly tacky. Place the dough in a lightly oiled bowl and cover. Keep the dough in a warm place to rise until it has doubled in size, 1½ to 2 hours. *(recipe continues)*

Butter a 9 × 13-inch baking dish.

Once the dough has doubled, punch it down to remove any bubbles. Roll the dough out on a lightly floured surface to a 14 × 17-inch rectangle. In a small bowl, mix together the brown sugar and cinnamon. Turn the rectangle so a long side is facing you. Brush the dough with the melted butter and sprinkle the brown sugar mixture over the butter, leaving a ½-inch border along the long side farthest away from you. Working from the long side nearest you, tightly roll up the dough,

ending at the bare ½ inch. Tightly pinch the dough together along the seam.

With the seam side down, slice the rolled dough crosswise into 12 equal rolls. Place the rolls in the prepared baking dish spiral side up in four rows of three. Cover and allow the rolls to rise until almost doubled in size, 45 minutes to 1 hour.

Meanwhile, preheat the oven to 350°F.

Bake until the rolls are golden brown, 25 to 30 minutes.

Meanwhile, make the icing: In a saucepan, melt the butter over medium heat. Once melted, continue to cook until browned, 6 to 8 minutes. Once browned, remove from the heat and add the vanilla, heavy cream, salt, and powdered sugar. Whisk until smooth.

Frost the rolls while still warm in order to allow the frosting to melt into the rolls. Slice apart and serve.

Great-Grandma Hirschy's Donuts

I never knew my great-grandma Hirschy well, but as a child, I knew about her yeast donut recipe. Passed down to many in our family, these donuts make a case for why you should make homemade donuts every so often. I used to say cake donuts were my favorite, but that's probably because that's all that we ever bought. Although it didn't happen that regularly, I'd sometimes get up early and help take livestock to market. If Grandpa was along, it meant we'd stop for donuts. They were gas station cake donuts, but I was always happy with the experience until I tasted my great-grandma Hirschy's donuts. What makes a yeast donut different than a cake donut is the flavor that develops during the rising of the dough. That means this recipe will take time and a good part of the day to finish. Sure, it's easier to go out and buy a box of donuts, but you won't want to after you bite into one of these. I remember one winter day when my dad, not known for baking very often, came inside from working on the farm. The snow falling outside had slowed his work, and he thought it would be a great day to make these donuts. With the smell of frying yeast dough in the air, we all knew we were in for a treat, and thanks to my great-grandma's recipe, you will be, too.

FOR THE DONUTS
1¾ cups whole milk, heated to 100° to 110°F
1 large egg, beaten
4 tablespoons unsalted butter, at room temperature
1 teaspoon vanilla extract
⅓ cup granulated sugar
4¾ cups all-purpose flour
2¼ teaspoons (1 envelope) instant yeast
½ teaspoon grated nutmeg
½ teaspoon ground cinnamon
1 teaspoon kosher salt
Neutral high-heat oil, for deep-frying

FOR THE GLAZE
2 cups powdered sugar
½ teaspoon vanilla extract
4 tablespoons blackberry jelly (see Note)
2 tablespoons whole milk

Make the donuts: In a stand mixer fitted with the dough hook, combine the milk, egg, butter, vanilla, granulated sugar, flour, yeast, nutmeg, and cinnamon. Mix on low speed until the dough becomes a shaggy mass, 2 to 3 minutes. Add the salt and increase the speed to medium. Mix until the dough is smooth, pulls away from the sides of the bowl, and clings to the hook, 3 to 4 minutes. The dough will be sticky.

On a lightly floured surface, knead the dough into a smooth ball and place it in a lightly oiled bowl. Cover and set the dough in a warm spot to rise until doubled, 1 to 1½ hours.

Punch the dough down and knead to release the air bubbles. Roll the dough out on a floured surface to roughly a 16-inch round about ½ inch thick. Use a donut cutter to cut 12 donuts and

(recipe continues)

holes. (Alternatively, use a 3-inch biscuit cutter and a 1-inch biscuit cutter to remove the middle donut hole.) Arrange the donuts on two baking sheets lined with parchment paper and sprinkled with flour.

Cover and let the donuts rest until they have almost doubled in size, about 45 minutes.

When the donuts have about 15 minutes to go, pour 4 inches of oil into an 8- or 12-quart Dutch oven and heat to 355° to 360°F. Set a wire rack in a sheet pan and set near the stove.

Working in batches of 3 or 4 (depending on the size of your Dutch oven), add the donuts to the hot oil. Watch the temperature of the oil and adjust as needed to keep it in the range of 355° to 360°F. Fry the donuts until deeply browned, 1½ to 2 minutes per side. Remove from the oil and set on the wire rack. Continue with more donuts, followed by the donut holes until all are fried.

Make the glaze: In a small bowl, whisk together the powdered sugar, vanilla, blackberry jelly (if using), and milk. Dip the donuts and holes in the glaze. You can glaze the whole donut or only one side. Allow the excess to drip off and return them to the wire rack. Once the glaze has hardened, serve, or freeze for long-term storage.

Note: Use more milk instead of the blackberry jelly for a more traditional glaze.

Biscuit Egg Quiche

— Serves 8 —

Egg casseroles seem to have faded into the background of our modern food landscape. Maybe it's the association with time-consuming preparation or the idea that breakfast should be quick and uncomplicated. Whatever the reason, I believe it's time to revisit the magic that is the egg casserole. This recipe draws inspiration from one of my cherished childhood meals: a simple creation using premade biscuit mix that our family often enjoyed as a quick weeknight dinner. With eggs providing a meal's worth of protein, and biscuits adding heartiness, this recipe makes for a satisfying meal. The real beauty of an egg casserole lies in its lack of strict rules. Whether you whip it up for a leisurely weekend breakfast, a brunch with friends, or a hassle-free weeknight dinner like my family often did, the result is guaranteed to leave you satisfied, regardless of the time of day.

FOR THE ROASTED BROCCOLI
2 cups broccoli florets
1 tablespoon extra virgin olive oil
¼ teaspoon kosher salt
¼ teaspoon freshly ground black pepper

FOR THE QUICHE
Nonstick baking spray
6 large eggs
¾ cup whole milk
3 tablespoons unsalted butter, melted
¾ teaspoon kosher salt
½ teaspoon freshly ground black pepper
2 teaspoons Dijon mustard
3 Quick Drop Biscuits (page 26), or 2 cups cubed bread
1 cup cubed ham
1 cup shredded Swiss cheese

Roast the broccoli: Preheat the oven to 400°F.

Place the broccoli on a large baking sheet. Drizzle with the olive oil. Season with the salt and black pepper.

Roast until the florets are beginning to crispen and char on the edges, 15 to 18 minutes. Set them aside to cool. Leave the oven on but reduce the temperature to 350°F.

Make the quiche: Grease a 10-inch pie plate and set it aside.

In a large bowl, whisk the eggs, milk, melted butter, salt, black pepper, and mustard until they are smooth. *(recipe continues)*

Crumble the biscuits into irregular pieces and place them in the prepared pie plate, or place the bread cubes in the dish. Add the broccoli and ham over the biscuits. Pour the egg mixture over and finish by sprinkling on the Swiss cheese.

Bake until the quiche is golden and puffed, 35 to 45 minutes.

Let cool for 10 minutes before serving.

Smoked Salmon Frittata

— Serves 8 —

I am lucky enough to have Grandma Alice and Grandpa live five miles from my farm. My entire life, Grandma invited the family over for each holiday but would never let us bring any food for the meal. Only recently, when we planned a Christmas brunch, I convinced Grandma to let me bring this smoked salmon frittata. Brunches can traditionally be heavy on casseroles and bread, so a crustless frittata is an excellent addition for a little bit lighter fare. The salmon is the perfect salty, smoky flavor for the egg custard base, and the earthy goat cheese adds a creamy texture that melds with the eggs. This frittata will surprise and satisfy everyone, just like it did for my grandma!

2 tablespoons unsalted butter
8 ounces mushrooms, sliced
1 onion, diced
Kosher salt and freshly ground black pepper
1 bunch kale, midribs removed, chopped
10 large eggs
¾ cup heavy cream
4 ounces smoked salmon
4 ounces goat cheese

Preheat the oven to 350°F.

In a 12-inch ovenproof skillet, melt the butter over medium heat. Add the mushrooms and onions and sauté until the mushrooms are browned and the onions are softened, 6 to 8 minutes.

Season with ¼ teaspoon salt and ¼ teaspoon black pepper. Add the kale and cook until it is wilted, 3 to 4 minutes. Once cooked, remove the skillet from the heat and set it aside.

Meanwhile, in a large bowl, whisk the eggs until smooth. Add the cream, 1 teaspoon salt, and ½ teaspoon black pepper.

Pour the egg mixture over the onion, mushrooms, and kale. Tear the salmon into bite-sized pieces and evenly distribute them into the egg mixture. Dot the top with goat cheese.

Slide the skillet into the oven and bake until the frittata is set and slightly jiggles in the center, 20 to 30 minutes.

Let the frittata cool for 10 minutes before serving.

Almost Healthy Granola

I didn't grow up with granola for breakfast. In fact, I don't think Mom made any until I was in junior high. Even then, it usually sat in a large Tupperware container in the cereal cabinet, and I don't remember thinking twice about it. For me, my granola love affair began as an adult. I quickly found that while the idea of granola is healthy, it can easily become more of a snack than a health food. But this granola is slightly healthy, a little bit sweet, and balanced with a higher ratio of nuts than oats. It's great on yogurt or a morning smoothie, but even better as a crunchy, guilt-free snack!

2 cups rolled oats
1 cup unsweetened coconut flakes
¾ cup chopped walnuts
¾ cup chopped pecans
½ cup pumpkin seeds
2 tablespoons wheat germ
½ cup virgin coconut oil, melted
¼ cup maple syrup
½ cup honey
1 teaspoon vanilla extract
1 teaspoon ground cinnamon
½ teaspoon kosher salt

Preheat the oven to 325°F. Line a baking sheet with parchment paper.

In a large bowl, combine the oats, coconut flakes, walnuts, pecans, pumpkin seeds, and wheat germ.

In a separate bowl, combine the melted coconut oil, maple syrup, honey, vanilla, cinnamon, and salt. Stir until it is a smooth syrup. Pour the mixture over the oat mixture and mix well. Pour the granola onto the lined baking sheet and spread into an even layer.

Bake, stirring every 10 minutes, until the granola is deep golden brown and toasted, 25 to 35 minutes.

Let the granola cool for 30 minutes before storing it in an airtight container. The granola will stay fresh for up to 2 weeks at room temperature or up to 3 months in the freezer.

Peach Cobbler Baked Oatmeal

— Serves 12 —

Baked oatmeal is an excellent option when you're looking for something easy to eat that's not from a box. The concept is simple: bake it ahead of time and it's ready to go when breakfast time arrives. But baked oatmeal can tend to be lackluster. To dress it up and make it a breakfast that you will wake up craving, why not make it with the flavors of a fruit cobbler? Instead of a sugar-laden cobbler topping, this baked oatmeal topping is only slightly sweet, allowing the peach layer at the bottom to shine through and, more importantly, make this a breakfast food.

Nonstick baking spray
4 cups sliced peaches, fresh, frozen, or canned (drained)
2 tablespoons sugar
1 tablespoon cornstarch
1 tablespoon fresh lemon juice
4 large eggs
2 cups whole milk
2 teaspoons vanilla extract
8 tablespoons unsalted butter, melted
½ cup unsweetened applesauce
½ cup honey
6 cups rolled oats
2 teaspoons baking powder
½ teaspoon kosher salt
2 teaspoons ground cinnamon
½ teaspoon grated nutmeg

Preheat the oven to 350°F. Grease a 9 × 13-inch baking dish.

In a large bowl, combine the peaches, sugar, cornstarch, and lemon juice. Stir to combine and dissolve the cornstarch. Pour the mixture into the prepared baking dish.

In the same bowl, whisk the eggs until they are smooth. Stir in the milk, vanilla, melted butter, applesauce, and honey. Add the oats, baking powder, salt, cinnamon, and nutmeg. Stir together and pour the mixture over the prepared peaches.

Bake until the oatmeal is set, 40 to 50 minutes.

Let the oatmeal cool for 15 minutes before serving.

Cornmeal Pancakes with Blackberry Sauce

— Makes 10 pancakes —

When we take the time to prepare food at home, it has to be worth it. Take the simple pancake; they should be easy to make, but we most likely reserve them for a meal at our favorite diner. There's a reason for that: getting perfect pancakes at home with flavor can be challenging. To refresh the classic pancake, this recipe incorporates cornmeal, which adds both sweetness and texture. The homemade blackberry sauce switches up the traditional topping of maple syrup for something much better: a sauce with just enough sweetness to heighten the flavor of the fruit and complement the pancake. With this nostalgia-inspired recipe in hand, home just became the perfect spot to get a diner-worthy pancake!

FOR THE BLACKBERRY SAUCE
2 cups blackberries, fresh or frozen
½ cup maple syrup
1 tablespoon fresh lemon juice
1 tablespoon cornstarch

FOR THE PANCAKES
1 large egg
1¼ cups buttermilk
1 cup all-purpose flour
½ cup yellow cornmeal
1 tablespoon sugar
½ teaspoon kosher salt
1 teaspoon baking powder
1 teaspoon baking soda
Butter, for frying

Make the blackberry sauce: In a small saucepan, combine the blackberries, maple syrup, lemon juice, and cornstarch. Stir to dissolve the cornstarch. Bring to a simmer over low heat. Cook and stir the blackberries, allowing the fruit to break down slightly, 6 to 8 minutes. Keep the sauce warm while you prepare the pancakes.

Make the pancakes: In a large bowl, whisk the egg and buttermilk until smooth. Add the flour, cornmeal, sugar, salt, baking powder, and baking soda. Whisk until smooth.

In a large skillet or griddle, melt 2 tablespoons of butter over medium heat. Add ¼-cup scoops of batter. Fry until bubbles form on top of the pancakes and the bottoms are golden, about 2 minutes. Flip and fry until golden, about another 1½ minutes. Once cooked, remove the pancakes from the skillet and serve, or keep warm in a 225°F oven. Finish making the pancakes, adding more butter if needed. Serve with the warm blackberry sauce.

Frances's Crumb Cake

— Serves 9 —

My great-grandma Frances was the first generation to live in my family's farmhouse. She would wake up early each day and walk to the barn's milking parlor, where she would do all of the milking by hand. I picture her returning to the house with a pitcher of fresh milk and then churning butter. While this was an undoubtedly arduous process, the convenient by-product of making butter is delicious buttermilk, which I can only assume she would have used for this coffee cake. The texture and flavor are exactly what you crave in a coffee cake, with a tender yellow cake on the bottom and a generous portion of streusel-like crumbs on top. Once you bake this treat, you'll see that Frances knew exactly what she was doing when she created this recipe.

FOR THE CAKE
Nonstick baking spray
8 tablespoons unsalted butter, at room temperature
½ cup packed light brown sugar
1 large egg
2 teaspoons vanilla extract
1 cup buttermilk
1½ cups all-purpose flour
½ teaspoon kosher salt
½ teaspoon baking soda

FOR THE CRUMB TOPPING
¾ cup packed light brown sugar
1¼ cups all-purpose flour
1½ teaspoons ground cinnamon
1 teaspoon grated lemon zest
8 tablespoons unsalted butter, melted

Make the cake: Preheat the oven to 350°F. Grease a 9 × 9-inch baking dish.

In a stand mixer fitted with a whisk (or in a large bowl by hand), combine the butter and brown sugar and whisk until the mixture is smooth and lighter in color. Add the egg, vanilla, and buttermilk. Whisk until combined. The batter will look curdled.

Add the flour, salt, and baking soda and whisk to combine. Pour the batter into the prepared baking dish and smooth it into an even layer.

Make the crumb topping: In a medium bowl, mix together the brown sugar, flour, cinnamon, and lemon zest. Pour in the melted butter and stir until the mixture forms into clumps like wet sand. Sprinkle the crumb mixture over the cake batter.

Bake until a skewer inserted in the middle comes out clean, 30 to 35 minutes. Let cool for 30 minutes before serving.

Dad's Cheesy Eggs

— Serves 4 —

Dad was often outside working on the farm before we woke up. That meant that if we woke up and he was in the kitchen, we were in for a treat with his recipe for cheesy eggs. He didn't cook much, but he loved making eggs with good cheese pulls. These are the eggs I remember him making, but with a few changes to ensure they're creamy and extra decadent. If he were still here today, I know he would have loved them more than the ones he made!

8 large eggs
2 tablespoons heavy cream
½ teaspoon kosher salt
½ teaspoon freshly ground black pepper
2 tablespoons unsalted butter
One 5.2-ounce package Garlic & Herb Boursin
    cheese

In a large bowl, whisk the eggs, cream, salt, and black pepper until combined.

In a large skillet, heat the butter over medium-low heat. Once the butter melts, add the egg mixture. Crumble half of the cheese over the eggs. Slowly cook the eggs by pulling in the sides as they set in the center of the skillet. Do not turn the heat up, or the eggs will overcook and become watery.

When the eggs are mostly set, 4 to 6 minutes, turn off the heat and gently crumble on the remaining cheese, allowing it to melt. Serve the eggs immediately.

Quick Drop Biscuits

— Makes 8 biscuits —

Years ago, when I told Grandma Conrad I wanted to learn how to make a good biscuit, she showed me her sister's recipe for drop biscuits. In Iowa, we have a different tradition for biscuits than in some other states, but that doesn't mean we don't love a fluffy melt-in-your-mouth biscuit. Instead of rolling them out and cutting individual biscuits, we simply portion the batter onto a baking sheet using a cookie scoop or spoon. The result is a perfect biscuit all thanks to Grandma's easy recipe.

2 cups all-purpose flour
1 tablespoon baking powder
½ teaspoon baking soda
1 tablespoon sugar
1 teaspoon kosher salt
8 tablespoons cold unsalted butter, cut into ½-inch pieces, plus 2 tablespoons melted for brushing
1 large egg
⅔ cup buttermilk

Preheat the oven to 450°F. Line a baking sheet with parchment paper,

In a large bowl, combine the flour, baking powder, baking soda, sugar, and salt. Whisk to combine. Add the cold cubes of butter to the dry mixture and toss to coat each piece in the flour. Using your hands, work the butter into the flour by pressing pieces of butter between thumb and forefinger until all the butter is worked in with no pieces bigger than the size of a pea.

In a small bowl, whisk the egg and buttermilk until smooth. Pour it into the dry mixture and stir together until it becomes a shaggy, wet, and cohesive mass. Use spoons or a ¼-cup scoop to make 8 equal biscuits and drop them on the lined baking sheet. Brush the tops with some of the melted butter.

Bake until the biscuits are raised and golden, 12 to 15 minutes.

Remove the biscuits from the oven, brush the tops with the rest of the melted butter, and serve.

Main Dishes

While compiling my family recipes for this cookbook, it got me wondering: are main dishes and side dishes still a thing? Do we still break down a meal into three distinct parts? When I look at the modern food landscape, I can't help but wonder if the traditional structure of dinner being a main dish and two sides still holds its ground in modern cookery. These days, many recipes seem to favor the quick and easy route: think one-bowl wonders that deliver a complete meal in a pinch. And you know what? I'm all for it. There's something liberating about crafting a whole meal in one bowl, especially when time is of the essence. But let's not forget about the classics. When I'm hosting family or gearing up for the holidays, I find myself gravitating toward the traditional main-dish recipes ingrained in my mind. The idea of a main dish flanked by two sides may seem like a relic, but there's a timeless charm to it.

In this section, you'll find recipes for both types of main dishes; from ones that will satisfy on a busy weeknight to others perfect for a slow Sunday supper. Take the recipe for Mom's Skillet Goulash Casserole (page 91). It's an unsung hero of quick weeknight dinners. On the flip side, some recipes in this section are reserved for the weekend when time is a luxury. Take The Best Pot Roast (page 77) as an example. The hands-on time is not extensive, but it spends hours in the oven. These dishes, while rooted in the past, are just as satisfying today as they were for our parents and grandparents. So, whether you're embracing the modern simplicity of a one-bowl meal or indulging in the comforting familiarity of a main-dish-with-sides dinner, I hope you enjoy these recipes.

Mom's Sunday (or Any Day) Meatloaf

— Serves 8 —

Meatloaf can be a contentious, hot-button recipe. You may love it. You might hate it. The idea could conjure up sour memories of dry, dense, and tasteless meat that you had to struggle to eat at the dinner table. For me, I'm fortunate to have happy memories when it comes to meatloaf. It was a cherished Sunday tradition thanks to my mom's love for it, so we had it rather frequently growing up. After rising early each Sunday morning to prepare the midday meal, Mom would set the oven to turn on while we were away at church. Inside, the oven was working its magic to cook meatloaf, potatoes, and, more often than not, green bean casserole. The moment we opened the garage door upon returning from church, the delicious smell of our lunch would envelop us. This recipe is a reimagined version of those cherished memories. It elevates the traditional meatloaf with the addition of fresh herbs and many cooked vegetables. The result is a meatloaf that will provide only good memories to anyone who tastes it. Guaranteed!

FOR THE VEGETABLE MIXTURE
1 medium onion, roughly chopped
1 rib celery, roughly chopped
8 ounces cremini or white button mushrooms, quartered
1 carrot, roughly chopped
4 cloves garlic, peeled but whole
2 tablespoons unsalted butter
½ teaspoon kosher salt
2 teaspoons minced fresh thyme
2 tablespoons tomato paste

FOR THE MEATLOAF
2 large eggs
1 pound ground beef
1 pound ground pork
2 tablespoons Worcestershire sauce
¾ cup panko bread crumbs
1 teaspoon kosher salt
¾ teaspoon freshly ground black pepper
⅓ cup whole milk

FOR THE GLAZE
¼ cup tomato paste
2 teaspoons light brown sugar
2 teaspoons Dijon mustard

Preheat the oven to 350°F. Line a sheet pan with parchment paper,

Make the vegetable mixture: In a food processor, combine the onion, celery, mushrooms, carrot, and garlic (work in two batches if necessary). Pulse the vegetables until they are finely minced, 10 to 15 pulses. (Alternatively, mince the vegetables by hand.)

In a 4-quart saucepan, melt the butter over medium heat. Add the vegetables and salt and sauté until the vegetables are cooked down and beginning to brown, 8 to 12 minutes.

Stir in the thyme and tomato paste and cook until the tomato paste darkens and begins to coat the bottom of the saucepan, 3 to 4 minutes. Once the tomato paste is cooked, remove the mixture from the heat and set aside to cool.

Make the meatloaf: In a large bowl, beat the eggs until smooth. Add the ground beef, ground pork, Worcestershire sauce, panko, salt, black pepper, milk, and cooled vegetable mixture. Stir

to combine and ensure the mixture is well mixed with no pockets of unmixed meat or vegetables.

Place the mixture on the lined sheet pan. Pat into a loaf, roughly 10 × 6 inches.

Make the glaze: In a small bowl, mix together the tomato paste, brown sugar, and mustard and brush the top of the meatloaf.

Bake until an instant-read thermometer inserted into the center reaches 160°F, 55 minutes to 1 hour 5 minutes.

Let cool for 15 minutes before slicing and serving.

Leftover Meatloaf Sandwich

— Serves 1 —

Now that you understand we had meatloaf most weeks (see page 30), it won't surprise you that my mom may have had a hidden agenda. And that was the ability to quickly create meatloaf sandwiches, one of her favorite leftover creations. There's a special kind of comfort in savoring meatloaf fresh from the oven, almost like the warmth of a grandma's hug, but, in our family, the real magic happens the following day when using the remnants of last night's meatloaf. Waking up knowing that a delicious meatloaf awaits in the refrigerator can make an ordinary day into a vastly better one. Once chilled, meatloaf thickens, making it easily sliceable. You can place it right on some bread, slather on the mayonnaise, and eat that happily. Or, for those seeking something a bit more elevated, consider upping your game with this recipe by searing the slice of meatloaf to achieve a caramelized crust, melting cheese on top, and generously spooning on this homemade secret sauce. Whether you've been making meatloaf sandwiches for years or think our family is totally crazy, try this recipe with our method and see how much you love it!

Note: Store leftover sauce in the refrigerator for 7 to 10 days.

1 tablespoon unsalted butter
One 1-inch-thick slice leftover meatloaf (see page 30), enough to fit over a slice of bread
1 slice provolone cheese
Meatloaf Sandwich Sauce (recipe follows)
2 slices bread
Red onion
Crisp lettuce

In a skillet, melt the butter over medium heat. Add the slice of meatloaf. Sear until well browned, 3 to 4 minutes. Flip the meatloaf over, and top with the cheese. Cover and sear until well browned on the other side and the cheese has melted, 3 to 4 minutes. Remove from the heat and set aside.

Spread as much sandwich sauce as you want on one slice of bread. Top with the meatloaf and cheese, onion, and lettuce. Spread the second slice of bread with some sauce, close the sandwich, and serve.

Meatloaf Sandwich Sauce

— Makes about ¾ cup —

½ cup mayonnaise
¼ cup ketchup
1 tablespoon yellow mustard
½ teaspoon onion powder
1 teaspoon garlic powder
¼ teaspoon kosher salt
½ teaspoon freshly ground black pepper
2 teaspoons fresh lemon juice
1 teaspoon Worcestershire sauce

In a small bowl, combine the mayonnaise, ketchup, mustard, onion powder, garlic powder, salt, black pepper, lemon juice, and Worcestershire sauce. Whisk until smooth.

Roasted Asparagus on Toast with Whipped Goat Cheese

Sometimes, a fresh take on a favorite can honor a time-tested tradition while providing something new that's even better than the original. This recipe is rooted in our family's creamed asparagus recipe, which came in handy when the asparagus patch overflowed in spring. I still make that creamed asparagus at times, but I find myself gravitating toward this more straightforward method as it highlights the flavor of the asparagus even better than the original. Roasting the asparagus leaves the vegetable crisp-tender and packed with fresh flavor. The whipped goat cheese spread adds a tangy, creamy layer against the rough texture of the toasted bread. And to round it all out, a jammy egg on top makes this perfect for both brunch and lunch. It's the same flavors I grew up on but with an updated, lighter approach.

FOR THE ROASTED ASPARAGUS

1 pound asparagus
2 tablespoons extra virgin olive oil
½ teaspoon kosher salt
¼ teaspoon freshly ground black pepper

FOR THE WHIPPED GOAT CHEESE

2 ounces cream cheese, at room temperature
4 ounces goat cheese, at room temperature
1 teaspoon grated lemon zest
1 tablespoon fresh lemon juice
1 teaspoon honey
2 teaspoons capers, drained and chopped
1 clove garlic, minced
1 tablespoon chopped fresh dill
1 tablespoon chopped fresh parsley

FOR ASSEMBLY

2 tablespoons unsalted butter
4 large eggs
Kosher salt and freshly ground black pepper
4 slices rustic artisan bread, toasted

Roast the asparagus: Preheat the oven to 375°F. Line a baking sheet with parchment paper.

Trim off the tough ends of the asparagus and place the spears on the lined baking sheet. Drizzle with the olive oil to evenly coat the asparagus. Spread in an even layer and sprinkle with the salt and black pepper.

Roast until the asparagus is crisp-tender, 8 to 10 minutes.

Set the asparagus aside. *(recipe continues)*

Main Dishes

Make the whipped goat cheese: In a medium bowl, combine the cream cheese and goat cheese and whisk until smooth. Add the lemon zest, lemon juice, honey, capers, garlic, dill, and parsley. Mix to combine.

To assemble: In a skillet, melt the butter and cook the eggs sunny side up, or to the preferred doneness. Season with salt and black pepper.

Spread the goat cheese mixture on a slice of toasted bread. Top with asparagus spears and an egg.

Roasted Pork Tenderloin with Spiced Apricot Glaze

— Serves 6 —

In our home, pork was a far more regular sight than any other meat. Whenever a recipe called for beef, my mom would find a way to use pork instead. Unfortunately, certain cuts of pork are often underrated by people outside of Iowa, mostly because they don't know how to properly prepare them to unlock their maximum flavor. If you're someone who's not super familiar with the meat, a tenderloin cut is a perfect place to begin your pork journey. This cut is small, cooks quickly, and retains its tender, juicy texture. The key to enhancing the flavor correctly is a dry brine. This recipe puts an updated spin on Mom's traditional dry brine, infusing the meat with tons of flavor through a mixture of salt, herbs, and citrus. Say hello to your newfound love of pork with this super-delicious tenderloin recipe!

1 tablespoon kosher salt
1 teaspoon grated lemon zest
1 teaspoon grated orange zest
½ teaspoon ground fennel
2 teaspoons herbes de Provence
2 teaspoons garlic powder
1 teaspoon freshly ground black pepper
Two 1-pound pork tenderloins

FOR THE GLAZE
¾ cup apricot preserves
2 tablespoons orange juice
1 tablespoon fresh lemon juice
1 tablespoon Dijon mustard
¼ teaspoon kosher salt
¼ teaspoon ground cloves

TO FINISH
2 tablespoons neutral oil

In a small bowl, combine the salt, lemon zest, orange zest, ground fennel, herbes de Provence, garlic powder, and black pepper. Mix together until it resembles wet sand. Rub the mixture over all of the surface of the tenderloins, using all of the dry brine. Cover and brine the tenderloins in the refrigerator for 1 to 2 hours or up to 4 hours.

Meanwhile, make the glaze: In a small saucepan, combine the apricot preserves, orange juice, lemon juice, mustard, salt, and cloves. Stir and bring the glaze to a simmer over medium heat. Simmer for 5 minutes. Remove from the heat. Measure out ¼ cup of the glaze into a small bowl. Set all of the glaze aside.

(recipe continues)

To finish: When ready to cook, preheat the oven to 375°F.

In a large ovenproof skillet, heat the oil over medium heat. When hot, add the tenderloins and sear until browned on each side, 3 to 4 minutes per side. Once browned, brush the reserved ¼ cup glaze over the tenderloins.

Transfer the skillet to the oven and roast until the internal temperature of the tenderloins registers 145°F on an instant-read thermometer, 14 to 18 minutes.

Remove the tenderloins from the oven, brush with more glaze, and allow them to rest for 10 minutes before slicing and serving with any leftover glaze.

Note: For an all-in-one meal, toss 4 cups broccoli florets with olive oil, kosher salt, and freshly ground black pepper. Roast alongside the tenderloin.

Iowa Pork Tenderloin Sandwiches

— Serves 4 —

I wouldn't be able to call myself a true Iowa native without including a recipe for a pork tenderloin sandwich in my cookbook. We take our pork tenderloin sandwiches seriously here, often judging restaurants on their version, with the most important criterion being how far they stretch past the confines of the bun. When my dad was still around, he'd drive us to a small town close by to stop at Crill's for one of the best tenderloin sandwiches around. As soon as you emerged from the car, you could smell exactly where you were. The intoxicating scent of a deep-fryer permeated the air. In no time, we'd be savoring large, crispy pork tenderloins with dill pickles piled on top, all precariously perched in a bun that was laughably undersized. Re-creating these sandwiches at home allows the recipe to be finessed for even more flavor. My version involves a modern twist, opting for a dill-infused dry brine. The dredging process uses pickle juice to further enhance that iconic pickle taste, with more pickles added on top for good measure. But one thing that remains sacrosanct is the use of crushed saltine crackers to coat the meat, ensuring that truly satisfying crunch. This recipe is your ticket to small-town Iowa for the quintessential tenderloin sandwich.

FOR THE DRY-BRINED PORK
1½ teaspoons kosher salt
½ teaspoon dried dill weed
½ teaspoon garlic powder
½ teaspoon freshly ground black pepper
2 pounds center-cut pork loin

FOR THE CUTLETS
2 cups crushed saltine crackers
1½ cups all-purpose flour
1 teaspoon garlic powder
1 teaspoon kosher salt
1 teaspoon freshly ground black pepper
½ teaspoon dried dill weed
1 cup pickle juice
½ cup buttermilk
2 large eggs
High-heat neutral oil, for shallow-frying

FOR SERVING
4 hamburger buns
Yellow mustard
Dill pickles

Dry-brine the pork: In a small bowl, combine the salt, dill weed, garlic powder, and black pepper.

Slice the pork loin crosswise into 4 equal pieces. Working with one piece at a time, place each piece in a plastic bag. Use a meat pounder to flatten the pieces into large flat cutlets ¼ inch thick. Once flattened, sprinkle all sides of the cutlets with the dry brine. Set on a baking sheet and place in the refrigerator for 2 to 4 hours.

Cook the cutlets: Once the pork has marinated, set up a dredging station in three pie plates. Place the crushed saltine crackers in one pie plate. In a second pie plate, whisk together the flour, garlic

(recipe continues)

powder, salt, pepper, and dill weed. In a third pie plate, whisk together the pickle juice, buttermilk, and eggs.

Working with one cutlet at a time, first dredge in the flour mixture, coating all sides. Next, dip in the buttermilk and allow any excess liquid to drip off. Last, dredge in the saltine crumbs until well coated.

Preheat the oven to 225°F. Set a wire rack inside a sheet pan.

Pour 2 inches of oil into a large cast-iron skillet or Dutch oven and heat to 360°F. Once the oil is hot, fry one cutlet at a time until well browned on each side with an internal temperature of 140°F, 3 to 4 minutes per side. Place the finished cutlets on the wire rack and keep warm in the oven.

Serve the cutlets on a bun with yellow mustard and dill pickles.

Sausage, Fennel & Apple Bierocks

— Serves 10 —

My earliest memory of bierocks involves Grandma Alice pulling them from the freezer to whip up a quick meal, be it for Grandpa to fuel him during harvest or for me when I made an unannounced visit. I realize that to me, bierocks are an everyday food, but you may have never heard of them. Grandma's recipe originated from my uncle's Russian Mennonite ancestors. They are a simple yeast dough that encases a filling to create a handheld sandwich. Think of them as a homemade Hot Pocket. Grandma had a knack for preparing large batches of these, ensuring a surplus in the freezer for those moments when a speedy, on-the-go meal was needed. This is homemade convenience food at its finest. The work spent making them fades from memory when you pull them from the freezer, warm them to perfection, and bite into the hearty dough. Nowadays, I make this bierock recipe more as a treat than for practical storage purposes. I've elevated the filling, introducing a blend of fennel, apple, a subtle hint of allspice, and sausage in lieu of ground beef. These flavors work together seamlessly with the traditional cabbage, a nonnegotiable ingredient in any authentic bierock. These bierocks have become my preferred accompaniment to a warm bowl of soup on a chilly day, serving as an apt sandwich-like side dish.

FOR THE DOUGH

1 cup whole milk, warmed to 100° to 110°F

2 tablespoons granulated sugar

2 tablespoons unsalted butter, at room temperature

1 large egg

3½ cups all-purpose flour

2¼ teaspoons (1 envelope) instant yeast

¾ teaspoon kosher salt

FOR THE FILLING

½ pound bulk sweet Italian sausage

1 bulb fennel, diced

½ onion, diced

3 cups shredded cabbage

1 apple, diced

1 teaspoon light brown sugar

¼ teaspoon ground allspice

1 teaspoon kosher salt

½ teaspoon freshly ground black pepper

Egg wash: 1 large egg, beaten

Make the dough: In a stand mixer fitted with the dough hook, combine the warm milk, sugar, butter, and egg and mix until the butter is incorporated. Add the flour and instant yeast and mix on medium-low until a shaggy dough forms, 1 to 2 minutes. Add the salt and continue mixing on medium until the dough is smooth and pulls away from the sides of the bowl, 4 to 5 minutes.

Place the dough in a lightly oiled bowl and roll it around in the oil to evenly coat. Cover the bowl and set it in a warm place to rise until it is doubled in size, 1½ to 2 hours.

Meanwhile, make the filling: In a large skillet, cook and brown the sausage over medium heat,

(recipe continues)

5 to 7 minutes. Add the fennel and onion and sauté until they are soft and translucent, 4 to 6 minutes. Add the cabbage, apple, brown sugar, allspice, salt, and black pepper. Cook until the cabbage is wilted and browned, 4 to 6 minutes. Set the mixture aside to cool.

Once the dough has risen, punch it down and knead it to remove the air bubbles. Portion the dough into 10 equal balls. Flatten or roll each ball into a 5-inch round. Add 3 tablespoons of cooled filling to the middle and fold the round

of dough over, creating a half-moon. Seal the seam using the tines of a fork. Place the prepared bierocks on two parchment-lined baking sheets. Cover loosely and place in a warm spot to rise for 45 minutes.

Preheat the oven to 375°F.

After the bierocks have risen, brush them with the egg wash. Bake until they are golden brown, 14 to 16 minutes.

Perfect Grilled Burgers

— Serves 8 —

The best part of my childhood summers on our farm was that there was absolutely no schedule. With daylight extending well into the evening, we found ourselves often losing track of time, tending to the garden or working in the fields until the sun dipped below the horizon dotted with growing corn stalks. Reflecting on those days, I'm amazed at how we still managed to gather around the table to share a meal. At this time of year, two favorites were on rotation: taco salad (see page 183) and these perfect grilled hamburgers. The grill was a godsend that allowed us to enjoy our favorite meals without heating up any appliances in the kitchen.

The secret to these hamburgers is beginning with high-quality beef and incorporating a handful of simple additions to amplify the flavor. It's a testament to the simple joy of summer evenings, where good company and exceptional food effortlessly converge.

1 tablespoon unsalted butter
1 small onion, minced
3 cloves garlic, minced
½ cup fresh bread crumbs
3 tablespoons whole milk
2 pounds ground chuck
Kosher salt and freshly ground black pepper
2 tablespoons Worcestershire sauce
2 egg yolks

In a small saucepan, melt the butter over medium heat. Add the onion and garlic and slowly cook the onion until it is translucent and beginning to brown, 8 to 10 minutes. Set the onion mixture aside to cool.

In a large bowl, combine the bread crumbs and milk. Mash them together into a paste. Add the ground beef, 1 teaspoon salt, ¾ teaspoon black pepper, the Worcestershire sauce, cooled onion mixture, and egg yolks. Mix together until well combined.

Form the mixture into 8 patties. Place the patties on a parchment-lined baking sheet. Use a large spoon to create an indentation in the middle of each patty about ¼ inch deep. Sprinkle the patties with salt and black pepper.

Preheat a grill to high for 20 minutes.

When ready to cook, turn the grill down to medium. Grill the patties for 2 to 4 minutes per side, depending on personal preference: 4 minutes per side for a well-done interior and 2 minutes per side for a rare interior.

The Best Herby Grilled Chicken

— Serves 4 to 6 —

Over my years of recipe writing, I've realized that not everyone feels at ease with the process of roasting a whole chicken. I get it: it's often more convenient to opt for individual pieces, perhaps relying only on chicken breasts rather than messing with dark meat as well. But I'm here to make the argument for the magic that happens when the entire bird is roasted. The thigh, packed with dark meat, offers rich, deep flavor that far surpasses leaner white meat. The legs provide an entirely unique eating experience, whether it's a child or someone who finds joy in savoring meat directly off the bone. Yes, Mom, I'm looking right at you. Consider this recipe a gentle nudge for those nervous about roasting a whole chicken. Think of it as an approachable step toward the Thanksgiving turkey but without the pressure. Packed with a blend of herbs, spices, and salt, the chicken will be flavorful and juicy. And when paired with a yogurt tzatziki, the recipe will become your favorite way to enjoy chicken. While this might mark your first time roasting a whole chicken, I can confidently say it won't be your last.

1 tablespoon kosher salt
1½ teaspoons dried oregano
2 teaspoons dried dill weed
1 teaspoon garlic powder
½ teaspoon onion powder
1 teaspoon freshly ground black pepper
1 tablespoon grated lemon zest
1 whole chicken (4 pounds), giblets removed
2 tablespoons extra virgin olive oil

FOR THE TZATZIKI SAUCE
¾ cup full-fat Greek yogurt
2 tablespoons extra virgin olive oil
⅓ cup grated cucumber, squeezed and drained
2 tablespoons minced fresh dill
1 tablespoon minced fresh mint
2 cloves garlic, minced
¼ cup fresh lemon juice
½ teaspoon kosher salt
½ teaspoon freshly ground black pepper

In a small bowl, combine the salt, oregano, dill, garlic powder, onion powder, black pepper, and lemon zest. Work the mixture together until it forms the consistency of wet sand. Set aside.

Spatchcock the chicken: Trim any excess fat from the tail and neck area. Set the bird breast side down. Use a sharp knife or scissors to cut along both sides of the backbone. Pull out the backbone and save for stock. Flip the chicken skin side up on the cutting board and press firmly on the breastbone to flatten the chicken as much as you can.

Being careful not to tear the skin, loosen the chicken skin as thoroughly as possible, getting all the way to the thighs and legs. Once the skin is

(recipe continues)

separated from the meat, rub the prepared salt/herb mixture into the meat, then on top of the skin, and finally on the underside of the chicken. Use all of the salt mixture. Place the chicken in the refrigerator uncovered for 4 to 6 hours to marinate. Keeping the chicken uncovered will dry out the skin and allow for more crispy goodness.

Once the chicken has marinated, preheat a grill to high for 20 minutes.

When the grill is ready, drizzle the olive oil all over the chicken. Place on the hot grill skin side down. Grill with the lid closed until the chicken skin is well browned, 12 to 15 minutes.

Turn the grill down to medium and flip the chicken over to continue cooking with the lid closed until the internal temperature reaches 160°F, 20 to 30 minutes.

Let the chicken rest for 15 minutes before slicing. During this time, the internal temperature of the chicken will reach 165°F.

Meanwhile, make the tzatziki sauce: In a small bowl, combine the yogurt, olive oil, cucumber, dill, mint, garlic, lemon juice, salt, and black pepper. Whisk until smooth.

Serve with the chicken.

Note: Alternatively, the chicken can be roasted in a 375°F oven for 45 to 55 minutes.

State Fair Marinade Grilled Flank Steak

— Serves 4 —

Much like pot roast, steak wasn't a frequent presence on our dinner table while growing up. Call me crazy, but to this day, I don't necessarily crave a classic steak. Rather, I find myself thinking about the flavors present in a good marinade, and how that can be the driver of a well-flavored dish. Over the years, I've honed my preferences for steak, recognizing that, as with most foods, the quality of the meat profoundly impacts the taste. Factors such as how the cow was raised, its diet, and treatment play crucial roles in achieving flavor and tenderness. But a high-quality steak meeting these criteria often comes with a hefty price tag, making it prohibitive for regular consumption. Enter flank steak. With its elongated, thin cut and pronounced graining, flank steak requires either a slow, patient cooking method or a quick sear with high heat. Personally, I prefer the latter. I always go back to the recipe in my mom's recipe box called "State Fair Marinade," although neither of us has any idea if it's actually from a state fair. The marinade works its magic as the meat sits, adding a rich complexity that pairs so well with a bright and vibrant romesco sauce. This duo of well-marinated steak and rich sauce has become my go-to choice, whether for a casual weeknight dinner or as an easily achievable centerpiece while entertaining.

FOR THE MARINATED STEAK

⅓ cup extra virgin olive oil

¼ cup soy sauce

2 tablespoons Worcestershire sauce

1 tablespoon Dijon mustard

½ teaspoon kosher salt

1 teaspoon freshly ground black pepper

2 tablespoons red wine vinegar

2 tablespoons fresh lemon juice

3 cloves garlic, minced

1 pound flank steak

FOR THE ROMESCO SAUCE

¼ cup unsalted roasted almonds

Half a 16-ounce jar roasted red peppers, drained

2 cloves garlic, peeled but whole

¾ teaspoon kosher salt

¼ teaspoon cayenne pepper

2 tablespoons chopped fresh parsley

2 teaspoons chopped fresh thyme

1 tablespoon red wine vinegar

1 tablespoon fresh lemon juice

2 teaspoons Dijon mustard

⅓ cup extra virgin olive oil

Marinate the steak: In a small bowl, combine the olive oil, soy sauce, Worcestershire sauce, mustard, salt, black pepper, vinegar, lemon juice, and garlic. Whisk to combine. Pour the marinade into a 9 × 13-inch baking dish. Place the steak into the marinade and turn it over to coat both sides. Cover the dish and marinate the steak in the refrigerator for at least 2 hours or up to 8 hours, flipping over once during the marinating time.

Meanwhile, make the romesco sauce: In a blender, combine the roasted almonds, roasted

(recipe continues)

red peppers, garlic, salt, cayenne, parsley, thyme, vinegar, lemon juice, mustard, and olive oil. Blend until combined and mostly smooth. The almonds will still provide some texture to the sauce.

Once the steak is marinated, preheat a grill to medium-high.

Remove the steak from the marinade and sprinkle with salt and black pepper. Grill the steak for 4 to 6 minutes per side, depending on preference.

Let the steak rest for 10 minutes before slicing. Slice across the grain on the bias and serve with the romesco sauce.

The Only Pizza Dough You'll Ever Need

— Makes enough for one 14-inch pizza —

There are two distinct types of pizza dough, each with its own strengths. The first is a straightforward homemade recipe reminiscent of soft bread with a subtle chewiness. The second is a brick oven–style dough featuring a higher water ratio that requires a slow fermentation process. There's a time and a place for this second type, but I grew up on the first, and it served as my entry into the world of yeast-based dough. What keeps me hooked on this bread-like dough is its user-friendliness; putting together the dough is super easy. Once pressed out to any shape, it is sturdy enough to hold any number of toppings, sauce, and cheese while keeping its characteristic texture. Even better, this dough can be prepared in advance and stowed away in the freezer before the rising stage. The night before you want to make a pizza, simply pull out the frozen dough ball, allow it to thaw, and let it rise overnight in the refrigerator. Complete the pizza with your preferred toppings, and voilà: pizza night is effortlessly made!

1 cup warm water, warmed to 110°F
1 teaspoon kosher salt
3 tablespoons extra virgin olive oil
2½ cups all-purpose flour
2¼ teaspoons (1 envelope) instant yeast

In a large bowl, combine the water, salt, and 2 tablespoons of the olive oil and stir to dissolve the salt. Add the flour and instant yeast and mix the flour into the water to form a wet and shaggy dough.

Knead the dough until it forms a cohesive mass. The dough will be slightly sticky.

Add the remaining 1 tablespoon olive oil to a medium bowl and roll the prepared dough in the oil, coating it completely. Cover and allow the dough to rise in a warm place for 45 minutes to 1 hour, or until doubled in size. Use with Taco Pizza (page 59); Garlic Butter Cheese Pizza Sticks (page 65); Sausage, Pesto & Spinach Braided Pizza Roll (page 66); or roll to a 14-inch round, layer with your desired toppings, and bake at 400°F for 18 to 23 minutes.

Taco Pizza

Growing up, I never thought it was weird that our go-to take-out pizza came from the gas station. And, there was only one no-brainer choice when it came to pizza, and that was taco pizza. It wasn't until high school that I realized you could actually whip up this recipe at home, and I've been doing it ever since. I think of taco ingredients like the cool kids in the kitchen; they can fit in anywhere. When you add them to pizza, the results are next-level. Forget regular sauce; we're talking creamy refried beans spiced up with seasoning slathered onto the dough. Then, it's kicked it up a notch with chorizo sausage and a hearty sprinkle of cheese. Once it's out of the oven, this pizza is basically a blank canvas in need of toppings. You can go wild with whatever your heart desires: lettuce, salsa, avocado, hot sauce, sour cream. Just like tacos, it's an "anything goes" kind of situation.

Pizza Dough (page 56)
1 tablespoon extra virgin olive oil (optional)
1 cup refried beans
2 teaspoons chili powder
1 tablespoon lime juice
½ pound fresh chorizo sausage, cooked
½ cup diced onion
2 cups grated pepper Jack cheese

FOR THE TOPPINGS
Lettuce
Salsa
Tortilla chips, crushed
Avocado

Make the pizza dough and let it rise as directed.

Position a rack in the bottom third of the oven and preheat the oven to 400°F. If you have a pizza steel (see Note), place it in the oven to preheat.

If you don't have a pizza steel, brush the olive oil on a large pizza pan. If using a pizza steel, the dough can be prepared on a pizza peel. Roll the prepared dough into a 14-inch round and transfer to the pizza pan or pizza peel.

In a small bowl, combine the refried beans, chili powder, and lime juice. Spread the bean mixture over the pizza dough, leaving 1 inch of crust around the edges.

Sprinkle the cooked chorizo sausage, diced onion, and pepper Jack over the refried bean mixture. *(recipe continues)*

Transfer the pan to the oven (or slide the pizza onto the baking steel). Bake the pizza until the cheese is melted and the crust is golden brown, 18 to 23 minutes. Let cool for 5 minutes before slicing.

Serve with chopped lettuce, salsa, crushed tortilla chips, and avocado on top.

Note: A pizza steel will give a more artisan-style pizza when the pizza is baked directly on the steel without a pan.

Christmas Lasagna

— Serves 12 to 15 —

For years, the Conrad family Christmas was synonymous with one dish—lasagna. This is my mom's side of the family, and I would look forward to this meal all year long. We would all congregate at Grandma's, and the dishes would be divvied up among each of her children's families. Interestingly, the person who made that year's lasagna never really mattered because this recipe yielded identical flavors, creating a shared experience that focused on the dish rather than the preparer. Without realizing it, I learned that lasagna is a love language because it truly is a labor of love. This recipe takes a few steps to prepare, but the smiles and memories made while enjoying each piece make it completely worth the time! So, whether you make it for your own holiday meal or any other day of the year, I know that this one will bring smiles to one and all!

1 tablespoon extra virgin olive oil
1 medium onion, diced
2 teaspoons kosher salt
5 cloves garlic, minced
1 tablespoon Italian seasoning
½ teaspoon red pepper flakes
2 pounds ground beef
½ cup red wine, like Merlot
One 6-ounce can tomato paste
One 15-ounce can tomato sauce
One 15-ounce can crushed tomatoes
2½ cups cottage cheese
2 large eggs, beaten
1 cup grated Parmesan cheese
½ teaspoon freshly ground black pepper
½ cup chopped fresh parsley, plus more for garnish
Nonstick cooking spray
10 ounces oven-ready lasagna noodles (10 to 12 noodles)
1 pound mozzarella cheese, shredded

In a 12-inch skillet, heat the olive oil over medium heat. Add the onion and 1 teaspoon of the salt and cook until soft and translucent, 4 to 6 minutes.

Add the garlic, Italian seasoning, and pepper flakes and sauté for 30 seconds. Add the ground beef and cook, breaking up the beef until browned, 8 to 12 minutes.

Drain off any extra liquid and pour in the red wine. Simmer until the wine is mostly evaporated, 2 to 3 minutes. Add the tomato paste, tomato sauce, and crushed tomatoes. Bring to a simmer and cook until slightly thickened, 6 to 8 minutes. Remove from the heat and set aside.

(recipe continues)

In a large bowl, combine the cottage cheese, eggs, Parmesan, black pepper, remaining 1 teaspoon kosher salt, and the parsley. Mix and set aside.

Preheat the oven to 350°F. Grease a 9 × 13-inch pan well.

Begin by layering 1 cup of the meat sauce evenly on the bottom of the pan. This will be a very thin layer, but it helps the pieces come out of the pan when removed. Layer noodles in the pan, slightly overlapping. The noodles may not be long enough for the pan, so a noodle may need to be cut to fit. It usually takes about 5 noodles per layer. Spoon half the cottage cheese mixture on top of the noodles. Next, add a layer of half of the meat sauce. Layer on half of the mozzarella cheese. Repeat the layering, starting with the noodles. Finish with the remaining mozzarella cheese. (Note: At this point, the lasagna can be covered tightly and frozen for up to 1 month. When ready to bake, let thaw in the refrigerator for 8 hours.)

Cover and bake for 30 minutes. Uncover and finish baking until it is bubbling and the noodles are tender when pierced with a knife, an additional 20 to 30 minutes.

Let cool for 15 to 20 minutes before cutting into pieces and serving.

Garlic Butter Cheese Pizza Sticks

— Serves 6 to 8 —

This feels wrong to say, but I trust that since we're all friends, it's safe to share a bit of embarrassing nostalgia. When I was growing up, buffets were viewed as a treat, at least in our family. Reflecting now, I recognize the privilege of enjoying homemade meals daily. However, during those formative years, it felt somewhat unfair that we predominantly ate at home while a wave of buffet restaurants were popping up in the '90s. Dining out was reserved for special occasions in our family, such as birthdays or at the end of harvest, but when we did dine out, Mom wanted to get her money's worth by visiting a buffet. My favorite standout was always the pizza buffet, which featured a pie filled almost edge to edge with cheese, its crust nearly caramelized, and cut into sticks. The faint aroma of garlic butter in the air still makes me smile. This recipe aims to re-create, and let's be honest, likely surpass my beloved buffet classic.

Note: While it is optional, serving with a side of marinara sauce will make these cheese sticks even better.

Pizza Dough (page 56)
2 tablespoons unsalted butter
2 cloves garlic, minced
2 teaspoons Italian seasoning
½ teaspoon kosher salt
1 tablespoon extra virgin olive oil
2 cups shredded Monterey Jack cheese
½ cup grated Parmesan cheese

Make the pizza dough and let rise as directed.

Position a rack in the lower third of the oven and preheat the oven to 375°F.

In a small saucepan, combine the butter, garlic, Italian seasoning, and salt. Melt the butter over medium-low heat. Once melted, remove from the heat.

Add the olive oil to a 12-inch cast-iron or other ovenproof skillet. Roll or stretch the dough into the skillet, spreading it to the edges. Stir the garlic/herb butter and brush over the dough to the edge. Sprinkle with the Monterey Jack and Parmesan.

Bake until the cheese is golden brown, 18 to 22 minutes.

Let cool for 5 minutes before slicing and serving.

Sausage, Pesto & Spinach Braided Pizza Roll

— Serves 6 to 8 —

When I was a very young child, I somehow convinced my mom to let me experiment in the kitchen. I vividly recall painstakingly painting mint leaves with chocolate, a process I'm sure that I saw Martha Stewart do, so I could place chocolate leaves on my cakes. I'd run out to the garden to get anything I could scrounge for a pizza, forgoing the usual pizza toppings for something a bit more experimental. All the while, Mom barely said a word except to provide some much-needed guidance. But I'm not here just to recount some of my random childhood escapades. These times of creativity fostered by Mom allowed me to craft unique creations, like this sausage, pesto, and spinach pizza variation. I've been honing this recipe for years, refining it until it earned a permanent place in my regular meal rotation. What makes it truly special is the way pesto works with sausage. Both have robust flavors but don't overpower one another when combined. Making this in a braided roll not only allows for more filling but also offers a fuss-free dining experience, whether enjoyed with your fingers or a fork.

Pizza Dough (page 56)
½ pound bulk sweet Italian sausage
½ cup diced red onion
½ cup basil pesto
6 ounces frozen spinach, thawed and squeezed dry
½ cup toasted pine nuts
8 ounces fresh mozzarella cheese, sliced
½ cup crumbled feta cheese

Make the pizza dough and let rise as directed.

Preheat the oven to 375°F.

In a skillet, brown the sausage and red onion over medium heat, 8 to 12 minutes. Remove the pan from the heat, pour off any juices, and set the sausage mixture aside to cool.

Roll the prepared pizza dough out on a piece of parchment to a rectangle about 15 × 12 inches. With a short side facing you, visually divide the dough into three vertical sections 4 inches wide. Spread the prepared pesto down the middle, leaving about 4 inches on each side. Evenly add the cooled sausage, prepared spinach, pine nuts, mozzarella slices, and feta on top of the pesto.

On the two empty sides of the dough, create strips by cutting from the edge of the filling to the edge of the dough into 1-inch-wide strips. Beginning with one side of the strips, lay a piece over the filling, then cross it diagonally with the opposing side, creating a braid. Repeat this until the braided pizza roll is formed. Transfer the pizza roll to a sheet pan.

Bake until the braid is golden, 40 to 45 minutes.

Let cool for 5 minutes before slicing and serving.

Skillet Taco Cornbread Casserole

— Serves 6 —

During my younger years, eating anything bearing the name "taco" felt like taking an indulgent trip to a foreign country. Before passing too much judgment, it's imperative to understand that living in my small Iowa town didn't afford me the luxury of exploring too many different types of food from around the world. Tacos marked one of the first departures from the familiar meat-and-potatoes fare that typically graced our dinner table. Since then, my sister and I have loved tacos, no matter the level of authenticity. The simple mixture of chili powder and cumin has the power to take humble ground beef from mundane to superb. While my mom often made a version of this recipe, I've enhanced the filling with a medley of fresh peppers, frozen corn, black beans, ground turkey, and additional spices. To cap everything off, a cornbread topping creates a crust that rivals a pot pie but surpasses it in deliciousness. This is the best casserole, and it's a testament to the magic that unfolds when you're exposed to something new and different!

FOR THE TACO FILLING
2 tablespoons neutral oil
1 medium onion, diced
1 bell pepper, diced
2 jalapeños, seeded and diced
1½ teaspoons kosher salt
1 pound ground turkey
2 tablespoons chili powder
1 teaspoon ground cumin
One 10-ounce can red enchilada sauce
1 cup sweet corn kernels, frozen or canned
One 15-ounce can black beans, drained and rinsed

FOR THE CORNBREAD TOPPING
2 large eggs, beaten
1 cup full-fat Greek yogurt or sour cream
½ cup whole milk
5 tablespoons unsalted butter, melted
1 cup sweet corn kernels, frozen or canned
⅔ cup all-purpose flour
½ cup yellow cornmeal
2 teaspoons baking powder
½ teaspoon kosher salt
½ teaspoon chili powder

FOR ASSEMBLY AND SERVING
1½ cups shredded pepper Jack cheese
Shredded lettuce
Avocado slices
Salsa
Chopped cilantro
Sour cream

Preheat the oven to 400°F.

Make the taco filling: In a 12-inch ovenproof skillet, heat the oil over medium heat. Add the onion, bell pepper, jalapeños, and salt and sauté *(recipe continues)* until the onion is translucent and beginning to brown, 6 to 8 minutes.

Add the ground turkey and cook, breaking it apart into small pieces, until browned, 4 to 6 minutes.

Pour off any extra liquid from the pan. Add the chili powder and cumin and stir to warm the spices. Add the enchilada sauce, sweet corn, and black beans. Stir and bring the mixture to a simmer. Reduce the heat to low while making the topping.

Make the cornbread topping: In a large bowl, combine the eggs, yogurt, milk, melted butter, and sweet corn. Whisk until smooth. Add the flour, cornmeal, baking powder, salt, and chili powder. Fold the ingredients together to form a thick batter.

Remove the skillet from the heat. Sprinkle the top with the pepper Jack cheese. Spoon the cornbread batter over the filling. Spread into an even layer.

Bake until the cornbread is set and golden brown, 18 to 24 minutes.

Let cool for 10 minutes before serving with toppings of choice: shredded lettuce, sliced avocado, salsa, cilantro, and sour cream.

Layered Spaghetti Pie

— Serves 6 to 8 —

Even now, the image of my mom seated in a chair, engrossed in reading recipe magazines, is embossed in my mind. *Martha Stewart Living, Country Woman, Taste of Home,* and *Better Homes & Gardens* were always lying around or in stacks by a chair. These magazines were a shared experience between my Grandma Conrad and Mom, creating some occasional contention over who would be able to read them first. More often than not, Grandma Conrad was the winner, and Mom, ever the dutiful daughter, waited patiently for her turn. The pages of these magazines were filled with rip-apart recipes that could easily be stored in a recipe box. I remember poring over the issues when they finally came to me, even though they didn't always feel very new, as they had already made their way through two knowledgeable cooks by then. But I wouldn't have had it any other way. In the '90s, many of these magazine recipes were designed to be quick versions of familiar dishes, much like this spaghetti pie recipe that I've never been able to forget. This casserole-like pie could be assembled in the morning and baked when you got back home for dinner. It was enchanting with a departure from our usual spaghetti made from home-canned tomato sauce. Over the years, I've added my own tweaks to the original recipe, and it now perfectly encapsulates every memory I hold dear about spaghetti pie. It's not just a dish; it's packed with nostalgia, family traditions, and, of course, great flavors.

½ pound spaghetti
2 tablespoons extra virgin olive oil
1 medium onion, diced
1 green bell pepper, diced
1½ teaspoons kosher salt
3 cloves garlic, minced
½ pound bulk Italian sausage
2½ teaspoons Italian seasoning
¼ teaspoon red pepper flakes
2 tablespoons tomato paste
Nonstick cooking spray
One 15-ounce can tomato sauce
3 large eggs
1 cup whole milk ricotta cheese
½ cup grated Parmesan cheese
2 cups shredded mozzarella cheese

Cook the spaghetti to al dente according to the package directions. Drain and set aside.

In a 4-quart saucepan, heat the olive oil over medium heat. Add the onion, bell pepper, and 1 teaspoon of the salt and cook until the onion is soft and translucent, 4 to 6 minutes. Add the garlic and stir until it is fragrant, about 30 seconds.

Add the sausage, break the sausage into small pieces, and cook until it is browned, 6 to 8 minutes.

Pour off any excess liquid from the pan. Add 2 teaspoons of the Italian seasoning, the pepper flakes, and tomato paste. Cook the tomato paste until it darkens in color and creates a film on the bottom of the saucepan, 3 to 4 minutes.

(recipe continues)

Stir in the tomato sauce, bring it to a simmer, and cook on low for 4 minutes. Remove it from the heat to cool slightly.

Preheat the oven to 350°F. Grease a 10-inch deep-dish pie plate or a 9 × 9-inch baking dish and set aside.

In a large bowl, whisk 2 of the eggs until smooth. Add the cooked spaghetti and cooled sauce. Stir to combine and pour half of the mixture into the prepared pie plate.

In a medium bowl, whisk the remaining egg until it is smooth. Add the ricotta, Parmesan, and the remaining ½ teaspoon salt and ½ teaspoon Italian seasoning. Stir to combine and spread evenly over the layer of spaghetti in the pie plate. Pour on the remaining spaghetti and spread evenly. Sprinkle with the shredded mozzarella.

Bake until the cheese is golden and the pie is bubbling, 45 to 55 minutes.

Let the pie cool for 15 minutes before slicing and serving.

Chicken & Biscuits

— Serves 8 —

Chicken and biscuits never felt like a special-occasion meal growing up. Looking back on it now, the fact that we didn't have it often must have meant it was a treat. To my child eyes, it appeared that Mom just threw together a few ingredients, and come dinnertime, we magically had a comforting dish of chicken with beautifully golden biscuits. While there's no actual magic involved, the outcome of this recipe is always perfect, and the secret lies in the filling. The vegetables are sautéed with butter for richness, flour forms a quick roux that's made into a silky-smooth sauce, and quick drop biscuits (yes, just like those on page 26) are dolloped on top and browned in the oven. This is a one-pot meal that eats like a feast, and since the filling and biscuits can be made and baked in an hour, I'd like to argue that this perfectly fits the bill for a weeknight workhorse.

FOR THE FILLING
4 tablespoons unsalted butter
1 onion, diced
1 rib celery, diced
2 carrots, diced
2 teaspoons kosher salt
1 teaspoon freshly ground black pepper
3 cloves garlic, minced
1 pound boneless, skinless chicken breast, cubed
2 tablespoons minced fresh sage
1 tablespoon minced fresh thyme
4 tablespoons all-purpose flour
½ cup white wine (optional)
1 cup whole milk
2 cups chicken stock

FOR THE BISCUITS
2 cups all-purpose flour
1 tablespoon baking powder
½ teaspoon baking soda
2 teaspoons minced fresh thyme
1 teaspoon kosher salt
8 tablespoons unsalted butter, cubed and chilled
1 cup shredded cheddar cheese
1 large egg
⅔ cup buttermilk

Make the filling: In a 6-quart ovenproof saucepan or Dutch oven, melt the butter over medium heat. Add the onion, celery, carrots, salt, and black pepper and cook until the onion is soft and beginning to brown, 6 to 8 minutes. Add the garlic and sauté until fragrant, about 30 seconds. Add the cubed chicken and cook until the chicken is fully cooked, 8 to 10 minutes.

Stir in the sage and thyme. Add the white wine (if using) and cook until evaporated, 1 to 2 minutes.

(recipe continues)

Sprinkle the flour over the mixture, stir, and cook until it forms a roux, 1 to 2 minutes. Slowly pour in the milk and stir until smooth. Pour in the chicken stock and bring the mixture to a simmer. Cook until the mixture is slightly thickened and bubbling, 4 to 6 minutes. Once thickened, turn off the heat and make the biscuits.

Preheat the oven to 450°F.

Make the biscuits: In a large bowl, mix the flour, baking powder, baking soda, thyme, and salt. Toss in the butter cubes, coating each piece in the flour. Work the butter into the flour by pressing pieces of butter between thumb and forefinger until all the butter is worked in with no pieces bigger than the size of a pea. Toss the cheddar into the dry mixture.

In a small bowl, whisk the egg and buttermilk until smooth. Pour the mixture into the dry mixture and stir everything together until it becomes a shaggy, wet, and cohesive mass. Use spoons or a ¼-cup scoop to make 8 equal biscuits on top of the chicken mixture.

Bake until the biscuits are golden, 12 to 15 minutes.

Let cool for 10 to 15 minutes before serving.

The Best Pot Roast

— Serves 6 to 8 —

Beef was a once-in-a-while sighting on our family dinner table when I was growing up. Even dishes that typically called for ground beef in their ingredient list, like casseroles, were swapped for ground pork. We raised pork and had a freezer full of various cuts, so we had plenty available to use in most recipes. My parents considered beef a treat; something special, so it showed up only occasionally. To put it in perspective, Grandma and Grandpa, in their generosity, would at times gift each family a quarter of beef for Christmas. That was a big deal, and we treated that beef like gold. Maybe it was the scarcity or just my taste buds, but I never found myself craving beef. Well, except for one thing: Mom's pot roast. My take on this recipe kicks the flavor up a notch, borrowing a few moves from another classic, beef bourguignon, to give the meat a deep, rich taste. The lengthy oven time is completely intentional and is the secret to the most tender meat you've ever had. But here's one tip for a better dish: wait to throw in the vegetables until the end of the roasting. It keeps them crisp-tender, and in my book, that's the way they should be. Pot roast may sound a bit old-fashioned, but it's homey and comforting and a delicious treat.

3 to 4 pounds beef chuck roast
1 tablespoon kosher salt
1 teaspoon freshly ground black pepper
2 tablespoons neutral oil
2 tablespoons unsalted butter
1 small onion, diced
2 carrots, diced
2 ribs celery, diced
2 tablespoons tomato paste
1 cup red wine
3 cups beef stock
2 tablespoons Worcestershire sauce
3 bay leaves
2 sprigs fresh thyme
2 sprigs fresh rosemary
1 head garlic
1½ pounds carrots, cut into sticks
1½ pounds small yellow potatoes (if using large, cut into bite-sized pieces)
1 tablespoon cornstarch

Preheat the oven to 325°F.

Sprinkle the entire chuck roast all over with the salt and black pepper. In an 8-quart Dutch oven, heat the oil over medium heat. Once hot, sear the roast until deeply browned on two sides, 4 to 6 minutes per side. Remove from the Dutch oven and blot out the excess oil with a paper towel.

In the same Dutch oven, melt the butter over medium heat. Add the onion, carrots, and celery and sauté until soft and beginning to brown on the bottom of the Dutch oven, 6 to 8 minutes.

Add the tomato paste and cook until the paste forms a caramelized layer, about 3 minutes. Add the red wine, beef stock, Worcestershire sauce, bay leaves, thyme, and rosemary.

(recipe continues)

Place the chuck roast in the middle of the liquid in the Dutch oven. Keeping the bulb intact, cut the top one-quarter off the head of garlic, exposing the cloves. Place the head of garlic in the Dutch oven with the roast.

Cover, transfer to the oven, and roast until it is fall-apart tender, about 1 hour per pound of meat, 3 to 4 hours total.

About 1 hour before the roast is done, remove ¼ cup of the liquid and the head of garlic. Add the carrot sticks and potatoes to the pot and return to the oven.

Continue to roast until the carrots and potatoes are tender, 45 minutes to 1 hour.

Remove the pot from the oven and remove the roast, carrots, and potatoes, leaving the liquid in the pan.

Set the pan over medium heat. Squeeze the roasted garlic cloves into the pot. Whisk the cornstarch into the reserved cooled liquid. Stir this cornstarch slurry into the hot drippings and cook until slightly thickened like gravy, 3 to 4 minutes.

Serve the roast and vegetables with the gravy.

Leftover Pot Roast Sandwiches
(aka Beef Salad)

— Serves 4 —

Now that my love for a good pot roast is known (check out the recipe on page 77), let's talk about the part I may like even better—the leftovers. When a dish is slow-cooked at a low temperature, the flavors deepen and somehow become even more amazing the next day. I do understand that whipping up a whole pot roast just for leftovers isn't the best idea, but this sandwich is so tasty that you might need to hide away part of the roast or even make a second one. I think the whole leftovers-turned-sandwich idea probably started when pot roasts were more of a regular thing, and not what we now consider an elevated dinner. Some ingenious person in their kitchen must have realized that the pot roast leftovers could be their own magical recipe, and the "beef salad" was born. The name doesn't do justice to this sandwich masterpiece, but that's what my mom always called it. I still believe she'd secretly tuck it into the back of the refrigerator and enjoy it for lunch while I was stuck in school. She denies it, of course. The recipe is simple, and if you have time, it is completely worth the extra step of making the homemade mayonnaise. All you need to finish this off is some slices of high-quality bread and crunchy lettuce. Your pot roast leftovers just got a seriously delicious makeover.

½ pound Best Pot Roast (page 77), shredded
½ cup Homemade Mayonnaise (recipe follows)
1 hard-boiled egg, diced
2 tablespoons sweet pickle relish
¼ teaspoon kosher salt
¼ teaspoon freshly ground black pepper
8 slices bread
Red onion slices
Crisp lettuce

In a bowl, combine the beef, mayonnaise, egg, relish, salt, and black pepper. Mix until combined. Spread generously on bread and top with red onion slices and lettuce.

Homemade Mayonnaise

— Makes about 1 cup —

1 large egg
1 teaspoon Dijon mustard
1 teaspoon fresh lemon juice
½ teaspoon kosher salt
1 cup neutral oil

In a blender or food processor, combine the egg, mustard, lemon juice, and salt. With the blender running slowly, drizzle in the oil until the mayonnaise is thick, 1 to 2 minutes.

Store any leftover mayonnaise in an airtight container in the refrigerator for up to 2 weeks.

Crispy Oven-Fried Chicken Tenders

— Serves 4 to 6 —

Do you ever catch yourself reminiscing about the dishes you craved as a kid, only to grow up and question your younger self's cravings? Am I the only one in this boat? I used to be all about those compressed, thinly breaded, and slightly soggy chicken nuggets back in the day. Real meat or not, I thought they were the epitome of good food. I remember one time Mom brought some home from the store, and it was like we hit the food lottery. Sure, the store-bought options today are most likely better than when I was young—I think they use real meat now—but there's something special about homemade ones. The funny thing is, homemade ones are way better than their processed alternatives, and I think on some level I knew that even as a child. So, when I decided to create my own chicken tenders recipe, my goal was simple: make something my nieces and nephew would gladly eat. Luckily for me, they love these! They're crispy, craggily breaded pieces of chicken that are seasoned to perfection. If only I had known and could have appreciated how awesome these were back in the day!

FOR THE DRY RUB

1½ teaspoons smoked paprika
1½ teaspoons garlic powder
¾ teaspoon onion powder
¼ teaspoon cayenne pepper
1½ teaspoons kosher salt
½ teaspoon freshly ground black pepper

FOR THE CHICKEN TENDERS

2 pounds boneless, skinless chicken breasts, patted dry
¾ cup all-purpose flour
3 cups crushed cornflakes
½ cup buttermilk
1 large egg
Buttermilk Ranch Dressing (page 182), for serving

Make the dry rub: In a small bowl, combine the smoked paprika, garlic powder, onion powder, cayenne, salt, and black pepper. Mix to combine and set it aside.

Prepare the chicken: Slice each of the chicken breasts into 3 or 4 pieces. Sprinkle all sides of the chicken pieces with the dry rub, using all of the mixture. Cover and place the prepared chicken tenders in the refrigerator to marinate for at least 2 and up to 4 hours.

When ready to cook, preheat the oven to 375°F. Set a wire rack in a sheet pan.

Set up a dredging station in three shallow dishes: Spread the flour in one dish. Spread the crushed cornflakes in a second. In the third, whisk together the buttermilk and egg until smooth.

(recipe continues)

Start coating the chicken tenders. Roll the tenders first in the flour to coat all sides. Transfer the floured tenders to the buttermilk/egg mixture. Dip them in the mixture and drip off any excess liquid. Finally, roll the tenders in the crushed cornflakes, coating all sides. Place the prepared tenders on the rack-lined baking sheet. Once everything is coated, place the tenders in the refrigerator for 30 minutes (this ensures the crispy coating sticks).

Transfer the pan to the oven and bake until the internal temperature of the tenders registers 165°F, 20 to 25 minutes.

Serve with Buttermilk Ranch Dressing.

Scalloped Potatoes & Ham

— Serves 8 to 10 —

Take a peek into any Midwest church cookbook, and you'll find a bunch of scalloped dishes. Not just the usual potatoes; you'll see recipes for pineapple and corn versions, too. For the longest time, I thought I had the whole "scalloped" thing figured out. To me, it was a casserole with added cheese. Turns out, what I always considered scalloped potatoes and ham was more like a mixture of scalloped and au gratin. Imagine my surprise! If you're curious, here's the distinction: scalloped potatoes are all about layering sliced potatoes with cream or milk. When you add cheese, you have au gratin. I know, it's not earth-shattering, but it was definitely news to me. It just goes to show that what's normal for any one of us growing up isn't always the standard. So, this recipe is for my version of classic scalloped potatoes, which may not be what you knew scalloped potatoes to be. If you're used to the French-style scallop (au gratin), these might throw you for a loop, but hopefully in a tasty and unique way. Try something new; I think you'll love them.

Softened butter, for the baking dish
3 tablespoons unsalted butter
1 medium onion
1½ teaspoons kosher salt
3 cloves garlic, minced
2 teaspoons fresh thyme
2 teaspoons minced fresh rosemary
⅓ cup all-purpose flour
3 cups whole milk
2 teaspoons whole-grain mustard
½ teaspoon freshly ground black pepper
1 cup shredded Gruyère cheese
1½ cups shredded sharp cheddar cheese
3 pounds russet potatoes, peeled and cut into ½-inch cubes
1½ cups cubed cooked ham

Preheat the oven to 350°F. Butter a 9 x 13-inch baking dish and set it aside.

In a medium skillet, melt the butter over medium heat. Once melted, add the onion and salt and sauté the onion until it is soft and translucent, 3 to 4 minutes.

Add the garlic, thyme, and rosemary and stir for 30 seconds. Stir in the flour and cook until it is foamy and creates a paste, 1 to 2 minutes. Slowly whisk the milk into the flour. After all the milk is added, bring it to a simmer and add the mustard and black pepper. Whisk the milk until the sauce is thick, about 2 minutes.

Remove from the heat, add the Gruyère and ¾ cup of the cheddar, and whisk the cheese sauce until smooth. *(recipe continues)*

Add the cubed potatoes and ham to the prepared baking dish. Pour the cheese sauce over the potatoes and ham evenly. Sprinkle the remaining ¾ cup cheddar on top.

Cover and bake for 30 minutes. Uncover and bake until the potatoes are tender and the cheese is browned, 40 to 45 minutes.

Let cool for 10 minutes before serving.

Calico Bean Tot Casserole

— Serves 8 —

This recipe is a nod to two of my all-time favorite comfort foods: calico beans and Tater Tot casserole. They were my mom's secret weapons for different occasions. Calico beans were a potluck hero, always there for last-minute invites or impromptu get-togethers. Tater Tot casserole, on the other hand, was her weeknight lifesaver. We had a strict "frozen tots only for the casserole" rule, and I'll admit, I pretty much piled them on my plate as high as I could since I never got them at any other time. This recipe, which combines the two, brings the sweet and tangy three-bean goodness of calico beans together with the ground beef and tots goodness of Tater Tot casserole.

Nonstick cooking spray
6 slices bacon, cut into small bite-sized pieces
1 onion, diced
1 pound ground beef
⅓ cup molasses
2 tablespoons yellow mustard
1 cup ketchup
1½ teaspoons kosher salt
1 teaspoon freshly ground black pepper
One 15-ounce can cannellini beans, drained and rinsed
One 15-ounce can kidney beans, drained and rinsed
Two 15-ounce cans green beans, drained
2 cups shredded cheddar cheese
One (32-ounce) bag Tater Tots

Preheat the oven to 350°F. Grease a 9 × 13-inch baking dish.

Line a plate with paper towels and set near the stove. Add the bacon to a cold skillet and set over medium heat. Cook the bacon until it is well browned and crisp, 6 to 8 minutes. Transfer the pieces to the paper towels to drain.

With the bacon grease still in the skillet, keep the heat at medium. Add the onion and sauté until soft, 4 to 5 minutes.

Add the ground beef, breaking the meat into small pieces, and cook until it is well browned, 6 to 8 minutes. Once the meat is cooked, remove from the heat and drain any excess liquid out of the skillet.

In a large bowl, combine the molasses, mustard, ketchup, salt, and black pepper and whisk the sauce until smooth. *(recipe continues)*

Add the cooked beef, onion, bacon, cannellini beans, kidney beans, and green beans. Stir until well combined. Pour the mixture into the prepared baking dish. Sprinkle with the cheddar and top with the Tater Tots in an even layer.

Bake until the sauce is bubbling and the tots are golden, 50 to 60 minutes.

Let cool for 10 minutes before serving.

Mom's Skillet Goulash Casserole

— Serves 6 to 8 —

Goulash, as I've always known it, is a hearty stovetop delight filled with macaroni, ground beef, tomatoes, spices, herbs, and cheese. Later in life, I came to realize that this Midwestern rendition is a departure from the traditional Hungarian goulash, which is more of a robust stew with meat and vegetables. Mom's skillet goulash, while different from the traditional recipe, has become a cherished classic in our family. Imagine it as a homemade upgrade to the store-bought box helper that we're all familiar with. That boxed version does the job when in a pinch, but it lacks anything extra special. The preparation for this recipe is just as straightforward, but the flavor is on a whole new level. A splash of red wine works wonders in building layers of flavor, and the addition of fresh herbs takes it from good to great. The beauty of it is that everything comes together in one skillet, allowing the flavors to meld and infuse directly into the macaroni. It's a perfect meal!

1 tablespoon neutral oil
1 onion, diced
1½ teaspoons kosher salt
3 cloves garlic, minced
1 pound ground beef
4 tablespoons tomato paste
½ cup red wine (optional), such as Merlot
2 tablespoons Worcestershire sauce
1½ teaspoons paprika
1 teaspoon minced fresh oregano
2 tablespoons chopped fresh basil
1 tablespoon chopped fresh dill
2 cups beef stock
One 15-ounce can diced tomatoes, undrained
1¾ cups macaroni
2 cups shredded cheddar cheese

In a 12-inch skillet, heat the oil over medium heat until hot. Add the onion and salt and sauté until the onion is soft and translucent, 4 to 6 minutes.

Add the garlic and sauté until fragrant, about 30 seconds. Add the ground beef and cook, breaking it into small pieces, until it is fully browned, 6 to 8 minutes. Drain off any excess liquid.

Add the tomato paste and cook until the paste begins to darken and stick to the bottom of the skillet, 3 to 4 minutes.

Add the red wine (if using) and cook until the wine is nearly evaporated, 2 to 3 minutes. Add the Worcestershire sauce, paprika, oregano, basil, dill, beef stock, diced tomatoes with their juices, and the macaroni. Stir and bring to a boil.

(recipe continues)

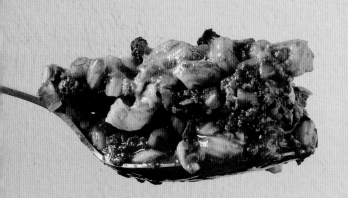

Reduce the heat to a simmer, cover, and cook until the macaroni is tender and the mixture is thick, 8 to 10 minutes.

Remove from the heat, add the cheddar on top, cover, and allow the cheese to melt, 2 to 3 minutes. Serve immediately.

Harvest Meal in the Field

Spring planting and fall harvesting were their own distinct seasons on the farm, with Dad and Grandpa working from dawn until dusk in the fields. Timing was everything: if the weather played nice, you had to seize the moment because, as we all knew, weather on the farm was fickle. Meanwhile, Mom and Grandma Alice played a crucial role in the daily routine, making meals for those working in the field. Sometimes, these meals were neatly packed and sent out, but at times, they were a bit more fun when we all headed out to the fields for a shared meal. If you're imagining a beautiful long table nestled under a large oak tree, it wasn't like that. These meals often took place in the bed of an old truck, hastily covered with a blanket to protect us from the dirt. Yet, despite the makeshift setting, the meals were nothing short of wonderful. Grandma Alice would sometimes pull bierocks from the freezer and let them thaw. These delightful bundles of dough (see page 45) were not only a personal favorite but also a convenient and time-saving solution when needed. It's funny how sometimes the simplest settings and meals can hold some of the best memories.

Side Dishes

Side dishes hold a special place in my heart, and I'll admit: I can turn any combination of them into a full-blown meal. They are where surprises in a meal can happen. Traditionally we expect certain things out of a main dish. But side dishes can be anything, and that's what makes them beautiful. They have the power to steal the spotlight or work as a team with other sides to create the ultimate holiday buffet. As much as I talk about our meals growing up, you would assume every night we had a perfect main dish and two sides. That was not the case. Often we had a main, but the other components of the meal were whatever was on hand, sometimes consisting of Mom's favorite summer side, pork 'n' beans, straight from the can. That's why when we did have sides that took more time, I enjoyed helping to create some of my favorite parts of the meal.

I've taken the classics, sprinkled in more flavor, and dialed up the texture to create some truly special recipes. Take, for example, the Roasted Broccoli & Cauliflower Salad (page 135). It's a nod to one of my all-time favorite church potluck salads. But in my version, I've elevated it by roasting the vegetables, infusing them with even more flavor, and turning them into a weeknight staple. So, whether you're piling your plate high with a smorgasbord of sides or choosing the perfect recipe to pair with a main, these revamped classics are here to make every bite a joy to eat.

Street Corn Zucchini Fritters

— **Makes 20 fritters** —

Church cookbooks adorned the shelves of our kitchen throughout my childhood, with Mom frequently pulling out one of the cookbooks for an evening's meal. I can vividly recall reaching for any number of spiral-bound books from local churches, flipping through the pages to locate specific recipes that had become a staple in our home. These cookbooks weren't limited to just our family's church, but spanned any number of nearby congregations. Each cookbook, packed with cherished recipes beloved by church members, became a warehouse of kitchen wisdom. The familiarity of these recipes is part of their charm; they are tried-and-true, approachable guides that taught not only me but countless others how to cook. One dish, zucchini fritters, came from the pages of a green cookbook with a black spiral. If my memory serves me correctly, it's on page 207. While zucchini cake and zucchini bread graced our table on ordinary days, these fritters were reserved for special occasions. Over the years, I've made batches, gradually adjusting the original recipe to include a hint of something special. The batter, though naturally simple, becomes fantastic with the addition of sweet corn and an assortment of spices. A notable upgrade is the chipotle-infused mayonnaise-based sauce, which is a vast improvement over the copious amounts of ketchup I used to use. The smoky heat of chipotle complements the sweetness of the corn and the richness of the cheese, resulting in a perfect bite.

2 large eggs
2 cups shredded zucchini
½ cup diced onion
2 cups sweet corn kernels, fresh or frozen
¾ teaspoon garlic powder
½ teaspoon kosher salt
¼ teaspoon freshly ground black pepper
1 cup all-purpose flour
½ teaspoon baking powder
⅓ cup grated Cotija or Parmesan cheese
2 tablespoons neutral oil
Chipotle Mayonnaise (recipe follows), for serving

Make the fritters: Preheat the oven to 200°F.

In a large bowl, beat the eggs. Add the zucchini, onion, and corn and mix to combine. Add the garlic powder, salt, black pepper, flour, baking powder, and Cotija. Fold everything together to form a wet batter.

Set a wire rack in a sheet pan and set near the stove. In a 12-inch skillet or griddle, heat the oil over medium heat. Once the oil is hot, scoop 1-ounce (or 2-tablespoon) dollops of batter into the skillet. Press the batter out into roughly 3-inch round fritters, leaving at least 1 inch between the fritters. Pan-fry the fritters, flipping once until they are golden brown on both sides, 3 to 4 minutes per side. As the fritters are finished, place them on the rack in the sheet pan and transfer to the oven to keep warm while you make the rest of the fritters.

Serve the fritters with the chipotle mayo.

Chipotle Mayonnaise

1 cup mayonnaise
1 teaspoon chipotle powder
½ teaspoon dried oregano
1 clove garlic, minced
1 tablespoon lime juice

In a small bowl, stir together the mayonnaise, chipotle powder, oregano, garlic, and lime juice.

Sweet Spiced Glazed Carrots

— Serves 4 to 6 —

The tradition of glazed carrots as a side dish for our Christmas Eve dinner began when my mom decided to designate this evening as a time for a special family meal, just the four of us. With Christmas Day reserved for extended family gatherings and a flurry of other festive events, having a dedicated time for our immediate family became a cherished tradition. Alongside one of our other favorites, party potatoes, glazed carrots earned their place on the menu after Mom made them and we couldn't get enough. While many classic recipes drown carrots in excessive amounts of brown sugar, I've reimagined my mom's version to showcase the carrots' natural sweetness. This updated recipe transforms the dish into something balanced and bright, featuring a touch of honey and orange juice that harmoniously enhances the carrots. Tossed in spices such as cinnamon, cumin, and ground ginger, the dish nods to holiday flavors while remaining versatile enough to be served on the table at any time of the year. They're a testament to the fact that traditions can be updated with success!

2 pounds carrots, peeled and cut into ¼-inch pieces
2 tablespoons unsalted butter
2 tablespoons orange juice
3 tablespoons honey
½ teaspoon ground cinnamon
½ teaspoon ground cumin
¼ teaspoon ground ginger
½ teaspoon garlic powder
1 teaspoon kosher salt
½ cup chopped fresh cilantro
½ cup chopped roasted salted pistachios

In a 4-quart saucepan, combine the carrots and ⅓ cup water. Bring the water to a simmer over medium-low heat. Cover and cook the carrots until they are crisp-tender, 8 to 12 minutes. Once crisp-tender, drain any remaining water.

Return the carrots to the saucepan and increase the heat to medium. Add the butter, orange juice, honey, cinnamon, cumin, ginger, garlic powder, and salt. Stir until the carrots are tender and glazed with a thick syrup, 4 to 6 minutes.

Remove the carrots from the heat and pour them into a serving dish. Sprinkle with the cilantro and pistachios.

Fresh & Bright Creamed Peas

— Serves 4 to 6 —

I have some great memories when it comes to creamed peas. My sister, Kelsey, not so much. She thought she was pretty unlucky when she was forced to endure this side dish. So, I get it that not everyone jumps for joy at the sight of peas, whether they're dressed in creamy goodness or simply tossed in butter. If you've never had the pleasure of trying creamed peas, they're essentially peas coated in a white sauce. This sauce can have any number of versions depending on who's in charge, but my mom's version was pretty straightforward: flour or cornstarch, water, and a pinch of salt. Shake those ingredients together, pour the mix into the peas on the stove, stir, and watch while they thicken. The one problem with this type of thickening is that it tends to be a bit bland and become pasty, especially when you're heating up any leftovers. So, I reworked the method to create a bright and fresh version that allows the peas to be enjoyed and enhanced with a lemony yogurt dressing. It's still super easy, but now it's totally worth the effort, and guess what? It's just as amazing, if not more when you sneak a cold bite the next day. Who knew creamed peas could be so tasty and something even my sister could enjoy!

1 tablespoon extra virgin olive oil
⅓ cup minced shallot
3 cups frozen peas
1 teaspoon kosher salt
½ teaspoon freshly ground black pepper
3 tablespoons heavy cream
¼ cup full-fat Greek yogurt
2 teaspoons grated lemon zest
1 tablespoon minced fresh tarragon

In a 4-quart saucepan, heat the olive oil over medium heat. Once hot, add the shallot and sauté until soft and translucent, 4 to 5 minutes.

Add the peas, salt, and black pepper and sauté until the peas are warmed through, 2 to 3 minutes.

Add the heavy cream, bring to a simmer, and cook until the cream is reduced by half, 1 to 2 minutes. Remove the pan from the heat and add the Greek yogurt, lemon zest, and tarragon. Stir to combine.

Serve immediately.

Roasted Broccoli & Corn Casserole

— Serves 8 to 10 —

I consider myself incredibly fortunate to have known my paternal great-grandparents, the visionaries behind our farm, which they established in 1947. The legacy they began continued through my grandpa and then passed to my dad. A big part of a farm is centered around food, whether it's what's being grown to sell or eat. I love imagining the meals Great-Grandma must have made in that very kitchen in which I spent my childhood. She managed four children, tended to the cows, dressed chickens, maintained a garden, and worked tirelessly on the farm, all while preparing daily meals. When I knew her, my great-grandma's time in the kitchen had dwindled, but I treasure the moments I spent flipping through her handwritten cookbooks. She knew what she was doing, to say the least. Among her recipes was one of my favorites: broccoli and corn casserole. Now, corn casserole is a staple here in Iowa, where scalloping pretty much everything is a bit of a tradition. Great-Grandma's twist involved adding broccoli, something so smart that I've since made it my own. I've updated the broccoli by roasting it beforehand for that perfect texture and flavor. A touch of Greek yogurt brings in a necessary richness. But, while I've changed many things in the recipe, I'm leaving the butter cracker topping untouched. It's sheer perfection, a testament to Great-Grandma's culinary skill that I wouldn't dare touch.

4 cups broccoli florets
1 tablespoon extra virgin olive oil
Kosher salt and freshly ground black pepper
Nonstick cooking spray
4 cups sweet corn kernels, canned or thawed frozen
4 large eggs, whisked
10 tablespoons butter, melted
1¾ cups butter cracker crumbs
½ cup yellow cornmeal
1 cup full-fat Greek yogurt
½ cup heavy cream
½ cup minced onion

Preheat the oven to 400°F. Line a baking sheet with parchment paper.

Spread the broccoli on the lined baking sheet. Drizzle with the oil and toss to evenly coat. Spread into an even layer and sprinkle with salt and black pepper. Roast until the broccoli is tender and beginning to brown, 16 to 18 minutes. Set aside to cool.

Leave the oven on but reduce the temperature to 350°F. Grease a 9 × 13-inch baking dish.

Using an immersion blender or food processor, blend 2 cups of the sweet corn until it is creamed.

In a large bowl, combine the creamed corn, remaining 2 cups corn, whisked eggs, 4 tablespoons of the melted butter, 1¼ cups of the cracker crumbs, the cornmeal, yogurt, heavy cream, onion, 1 teaspoon salt, and ½ teaspoon black pepper. Stir to combine, then fold in the cooled roasted broccoli. Pour into the prepared baking dish. *(recipe continues)*

In a small bowl, combine the remaining
2 tablespoons melted butter and the remaining
½ cup cracker crumbs. Stir and evenly sprinkle
over the dish.

Bake until the casserole is set, with the center
slightly jiggly, 50 to 60 minutes.

Caesar Roasted Brussels Sprouts

— Serves 4 to 6 —

I have a bad memory of my first encounter with Brussels sprouts. They were served at my school cafeteria straight from a can. No salt, no seasoning, just mushy, disintegrate-in-your-mouth Brussels. That experience left me with a serious aversion to vegetables from a can, especially when trying them for the first time. And that's probably why, to this day, I have strong feelings that anyone experiencing a vegetable for the first time should *not* have canned vegetables. But there's no better way to convince someone to love a vegetable than to serve it roasted. In this recipe, you simply toss the Brussels sprouts onto a sheet pan, douse with olive oil and seasonings, throw it in the oven, and the outside gets perfectly crispy while keeping the inside soft and tender. Plus, the high heat adds that sweet caramelization, which means even more flavor. While the sprouts are roasting, you can whisk together a quick tahini Caesar dressing, which elevates these Brussels from good to great, adding the flavors of your favorite Caesar salad to the crispy roasted sprouts. Forget any bad memories, because this recipe will change your mind!

2 pounds Brussels sprouts, trimmed and halved
2 tablespoons extra virgin olive oil
1 teaspoon kosher salt
½ teaspoon freshly ground black pepper
1 tablespoon unsalted butter
1 cup fresh bread crumbs
½ cup grated Parmesan cheese
1 teaspoon grated lemon zest

FOR THE TAHINI CAESAR DRESSING
2 cloves garlic, minced
¼ cup fresh lemon juice
1 anchovy fillet, minced
½ teaspoon kosher salt
¼ teaspoon freshly ground black pepper
⅓ cup grated Parmesan cheese
⅓ cup tahini
2 tablespoons extra virgin olive oil

Preheat the oven to 425°F. Line a baking sheet with parchment paper.

Toss the Brussels sprouts with the olive oil to evenly coat them. Lay them on the lined baking sheet in an even layer. Sprinkle with the salt and black pepper.

Roast until the Brussels sprouts are crisp-tender with browned edges, 30 to 35 minutes.

In a small skillet, melt the butter over medium heat. Add the bread crumbs and toss with the butter until the bread is toasted, 3 to 4 minutes. Once toasted, remove from the heat. Add the Parmesan and lemon zest. Stir to combine. Set the bread crumbs aside. *(recipe continues)*

Make the tahini Caesar dressing: In a bowl, combine the garlic, lemon juice, anchovy, salt, black pepper, Parmesan, tahini, oil, and 3 tablespoons water. Whisk until the dressing is smooth.

Drizzle the hot Brussels sprouts with the dressing and sprinkle with the bread crumbs. Serve immediately.

Sheet Pan Potatoes, Three Ways

We had baked potatoes almost every Sunday while I was growing up. It's one of my mom's favorite side dishes, but I'll admit, I was never a fan. I used to gripe about how dry and bland they were, always reaching for heaps of butter, salt, and pepper to make them somewhat interesting. Even with these additions, they still seemed dull. I must have been spoiled by those potato bar fundraisers at church, where you could pile on a mountain of toppings and create your own potato masterpiece. How could I go back to a simple baked potato after experiencing such endless possibilities? While we didn't exactly bring the potato bar home, we did shake things up occasionally by experimenting with different potato varieties and tossing in unique seasoning blends. To capture the essence of my potato bar memories, I've created three sheet pan potato recipes that hit the spot. Whether it's the Classic Sheet Pan Potatoes (page 114), the Buttermilk Ranch Roasted Potatoes (page 117), or Chili-Spiced Sweet Potatoes (page 118), each recipe embodies some part of the delectable flavors found at the potato bar, but conveniently packed into an all-in-one bite. The result is a roasted potato bursting with rich flavors, a perfect compromise for those days when you're craving the potato bar experience but don't have one at home.

Classic Sheet Pan Potatoes

— Serves 4 to 6 —

3 tablespoons unsalted butter

1 teaspoon garlic powder

1 teaspoon onion powder

½ teaspoon paprika

1 tablespoon Worcestershire sauce

2 tablespoons dried parsley

1½ teaspoons kosher salt

½ teaspoon freshly ground black pepper

1½ pounds russet or Yukon Gold potatoes, scrubbed but unpeeled

Chipotle Mayonnaise (page 101) or Buttermilk Ranch Dressing (page 182), for serving

Preheat the oven to 400°F. Line a baking sheet with parchment paper.

In a small saucepan, melt the butter over medium-low heat. Add the garlic powder, onion powder, paprika, Worcestershire sauce, parsley, salt, and black pepper. Stir to combine.

Cut the potatoes lengthwise into ¼-inch-thick wedges and place them in a large bowl with a tight-fitting lid or a zip-top bag. Drizzle with the seasoned melted butter, cover tightly, and shake the potatoes with the butter to evenly coat them in the mixture. Spread the potatoes on the lined baking sheet in an even layer.

Transfer to the oven and roast the potatoes until they are tender and beginning to brown, 25 to 30 minutes. Once browned, remove the potatoes from the oven.

Serve with Chipotle Mayonnaise or Buttermilk Ranch Dressing.

Buttermilk Ranch Roasted Potatoes

— Serves 4 to 6 —

1½ pounds russet or Yukon Gold potatoes, scrubbed but unpeeled

2 tablespoons unsalted butter

2 tablespoons powdered buttermilk

1½ teaspoons kosher salt

½ teaspoon freshly ground black pepper

½ teaspoon dried dill weed

1 teaspoon garlic powder

½ teaspoon onion powder

1 teaspoon dried parsley

Buttermilk Ranch Dressing (page 182)

Preheat the oven to 400°F. Line a baking sheet with parchment paper.

In a small saucepan, melt the butter over medium-low heat. Once melted, remove from the heat and add the powdered buttermilk, salt, black pepper, dill, garlic powder, onion powder, and dried parsley. Stir to combine.

Cut the potatoes lengthwise into ¼-inch-thick wedges and place them in a large bowl with a tight-fitting lid or a zip-top bag. Drizzle with the prepared melted butter mixture, cover tightly, and shake the potatoes with the butter to evenly coat them in the mixture. Spread the potatoes on the lined baking sheet in an even layer.

Transfer to the oven and roast the potatoes until they are tender and beginning to brown, 25 to 30 minutes.

Serve with Buttermilk Ranch Dressing.

Side Dishes

Chili-Spiced Sweet Potatoes

— Serves 4 to 6 —

1½ pounds sweet potatoes, scrubbed but unpeeled

3 tablespoons unsalted butter

1 teaspoon kosher salt

1 tablespoon chili powder

½ teaspoon ground cumin

¼ teaspoon cayenne pepper

¼ teaspoon dried oregano

Chipotle Mayonnaise (page 101) or Jalapeño Lime Dressing (page 185), for serving

Preheat the oven to 400°F. Line a baking sheet with parchment paper.

In a small saucepan, melt the butter over medium-low heat. Once melted, remove from the heat and add the salt, chili powder, cumin, cayenne, and oregano. Stir to combine.

Cut the sweet potatoes lengthwise into ¼-inch-thick wedges and place them in a large bowl with a tight-fitting lid or a zip-top bag. Drizzle with the prepared melted butter mixture, cover tightly, and shake the potatoes with the butter to evenly coat them in the mixture. Spread the potatoes on the lined baking sheet in an even layer.

Transfer to the oven and roast until the sweet potatoes are tender and beginning to brown, 25 to 30 minutes.

Serve with Chipotle Mayonnaise or Jalapeño Lime Dressing.

Make-Ahead Party Potato Casserole

— Serves 6 to 8 —

If you grew up in the Midwest, especially Iowa, you've probably crossed paths with the iconic "party potato." As Julia Child wisely noted, "A party without cake is just a meeting," and in the Midwest, we pretty much say the same about potatoes; if they're not in attendance at a special occasion, it's just another regular dinner. If you're asking yourself what a party potato is, no, it's not an extra-fun potato. Essentially, it's a potato casserole, but depending on who's making it, it can take on a life of its own. In my version, it all starts with mashed potatoes. Don't even try to use the boxed stuff; trust me, everyone will know. To soften its flavor and texture, garlic is cooked alongside the potatoes. Once mashed up, it's time for cream cheese, sour cream, butter, a splash of milk, and other seasonings. The extra fat content means you can make them a day or two ahead, store them in the refrigerator, and then pop them in the oven right before it's time to eat. They're utterly delicious, and the fact that you can prep them beforehand makes them even better. Party potatoes truly turn an ordinary gathering into something worth celebrating!

3 pounds russet potatoes, peeled and cut into 1-inch chunks
3 cloves garlic, peeled but whole
8 ounces cream cheese, at room temperature
¾ cup sour cream, at room temperature
1 cup whole milk, warmed to 100° to 110°F
4 tablespoons unsalted butter, at room temperature
2 teaspoons kosher salt
1 teaspoon freshly ground black pepper

In a 4-quart saucepan, combine the potatoes, garlic, and water to cover by 1 inch. Bring the water to a boil, reduce to a simmer, and cook the potatoes until they are fully tender and a knife inserted meets no resistance, 24 to 28 minutes. Drain the potatoes.

Mash the potatoes and garlic by passing through a ricer or food mill, beating in an electric mixer, or using a hand masher. Beat in the cream cheese, sour cream, warm milk, butter, salt, and black pepper. Combine until the cream cheese is fully incorporated and smooth.

Serve the potatoes immediately or save for later (see Note).

Note: If making ahead, pour the prepared potatoes into a 9 × 13-inch baking dish, cool, and cover. Store in the refrigerator and warm, covered, in a 325°F oven for 1 hour before serving.

Side Dishes

121

Sweet & Sour Stir-Fried Cabbage

— Serves 4 to 6 —

When I moved into my grandparents' house just across the road from my childhood home, one of my first moves was to set up a vegetable garden. Growing up, our large garden was chock-full of green beans, tomatoes, peppers, lettuce, spinach, broccoli, cauliflower, and cabbage. Without giving it much thought, I found myself replicating that familiar garden right in my new backyard. You may be wondering, with my mom's garden right across the road, why the need for such a sizable one of my own? Perhaps it was a bit excessive, but in my mind, it just felt right to plant my own. Over the years, the garden has grown more prominent, as has my love for cabbage. See, sauerkraut holds a special place in my heart, and you need lots of cabbage to make sauerkraut. I get it: not everyone shares my enthusiasm for fermented cabbage. But that's where my grandma's sweet and sour cabbage recipe comes in handy. It takes cabbage, adds a zing of tanginess, and balances it out with a touch of sweetness, sort of like sauerkraut. It's a simple recipe, but it's delicious enough that I sometimes whip it up as a side dish while entertaining. If by some miracle there are leftovers when everyone's gone—and trust me, I tend to make extra—I look forward to enjoying them as lunch the next day. More often than not, I find myself wishing I had just made the whole batch for myself!

6 slices bacon, cut into ¼-inch pieces
Neutral oil (optional)
1 onion, sliced
5 cups thinly sliced cabbage (about 1½ pounds)
¼ cup apple cider vinegar
2 tablespoons brown sugar
¾ teaspoon kosher salt
½ teaspoon freshly ground black pepper

In a large skillet, cook the bacon over medium heat until well browned, 6 to 8 minutes. Once cooked, place the bacon on paper towels. Pour off the bacon grease into a bowl. Measure 2 tablespoons of the bacon grease back into the skillet. If there is less than 2 tablespoons of bacon grease, add neutral oil as needed.

Return the skillet to medium heat. Add the onion and sauté until it is soft, translucent, and beginning to brown, 4 to 6 minutes.

Add the sliced cabbage and cook until the cabbage is softened and the excess water has evaporated, 8 to 10 minutes.

Add the vinegar, brown sugar, salt, and black pepper. Bring to a simmer and cook until the vinegar is mostly evaporated, 3 to 4 minutes.

Remove the cabbage from the heat, add the reserved bacon, and serve.

Sautéed Garlicky Zucchini

— Serves 4 to 6 —

Zucchini gets a lot of airtime during the peak of summer when the garden is practically throwing them out every other hour. Walk into a farmers' market, and you're bound to encounter zucchini in quantities the size of a mountain. Most people scoop them up by the armful, deciding to use them for sweet baked desserts. I'm all for a tasty zucchini cake, but there's something special about letting the vegetable shine in its natural glory. Getting zucchini right involves a few key steps. First, use small zucchini. Smaller ones will have fewer seeds inside and cook better without becoming soggy. And second, sauté the zucchini in butter, which browns it and gives it a crust, adding flavor. Last, do not add salt until the end. Salting early draws out moisture and steams the zucchini instead of browning it.

2 tablespoons butter

2 cloves garlic, thinly sliced

¼ teaspoon red pepper flakes (optional)

1½ pounds zucchini (see Note), cut into ¼-inch-thick slices

1 teaspoon kosher salt

½ teaspoon freshly ground black pepper

½ lemon

In a large skillet, melt the butter over medium heat. Add the garlic, red pepper flakes, and zucchini. Sauté until the zucchini is browned on both sides, tossing as needed, 8 to 10 minutes.

Remove from the heat and season with the salt and black pepper. Squeeze the lemon juice on top and serve.

Note: This recipe works best with small zucchini, which will have fewer seeds. If your zucchini are longer than 6 inches, first halve them lengthwise and remove the seeds before slicing.

Bacon-Fried Green Beans

— Serves 4 to 6 —

Over the years, our family has canned a ton of green beans. We're talking hundreds of quarts. Canning wasn't just a thing we did for fun; it was a sustaining life force in our family. With a large garden, Mom preserved everything she could to cut down on grocery bills throughout the year. If we grew it, we canned it. Despite the abundance of canned beans ready to eat in the basement, they're not a go-to craving for me. Mom, on the other hand, swears by them and might roll her eyes at my lack of love for them. So, what do I find myself craving? Fried fresh green beans. When the garden went bonkers and produced way more beans than we could ever possibly can, we'd eat on this recipe all season long. And the best part is the recipe is easy. First, steam the beans until they're just the right amount of crispy-tender. Then, turn up the heat, throw in some bacon grease (trust me, it's the secret ingredient), and let those beans sizzle and get a bit crispy around the edges. Even though it may sound like a hassle, this recipe truly is better when you use bacon grease. Growing up, we had a container of it right by the stove, and even today, I keep it in the refrigerator, always ready when needed. These beans are a speedy process and the whole family can never get enough of them. Every bite takes me back to those summer days, and honestly, that's the best part.

6 slices bacon, cut into ½-inch pieces
Extra virgin olive oil as needed
2 pounds fresh green beans
1 onion, sliced
1 teaspoon kosher salt
¼ teaspoon freshly ground black pepper

Place the bacon in a cold 12-inch skillet. Set over medium heat and cook until the fat is rendered and the bacon is browned and crisp, 6 to 8 minutes. Remove the bacon to a paper towel–lined plate and pour the grease into a small bowl. You need 3 tablespoons grease, so if necessary, supplement with olive oil.

In the same skillet, combine ⅓ cup water, the green beans, and onion. Bring to a simmer over medium-high heat, cover, and cook until the green beans are bright green and crisp-tender, 6 to 8 minutes.

Uncover and pour off any remaining water. Add the reserved bacon grease and continue to sauté until the beans are blistered and deeply browned and the onions are caramelized, 4 to 6 minutes.

Remove from the heat and add the reserved bacon. Season with the salt and black pepper and serve.

Old-Fashioned Cake Pan Potatoes

My grandma Conrad's world turned upside down in 1974 when her husband, Edwin, passed away from cancer. At the time, my mom, their youngest, was still navigating high school. The grief hit Grandma hard, altering her life in ways only serious loss can. Her cooking and baking slowed, but that didn't mean she stopped making food entirely. She continued to cook and can for the rest of her days. With her children gradually leaving the home, the need for large meals dwindled. Fast-forward to the moments I spent with her at my mom's kitchen table, where we bonded over canning sessions. It was during these times that I truly grasped the kind of cook Grandma was. She'd tell me all about the dishes she used to whip up when her kids were little, never bothering to write down the recipes. Everything just lived in her head with no need for instructions. Of all the recipes she shared during our kitchen chats, these cake pan potatoes are one of my favorites. They're similar to many scalloped potato recipes, using minimal ingredients to produce a dish that's both flavorful and tender, perfect for slicing into wedges to be served alongside any meal. The beauty truly lies in its simplicity. It's the kind of recipe that, like Grandma, you'll soon commit to memory and make your own.

Nonstick cooking spray
1½ pounds russet or baking potatoes (3 to 4 potatoes total), scrubbed and dried
1 small onion, grated
1¼ teaspoons kosher salt
½ teaspoon freshly ground black pepper
¼ teaspoon grated nutmeg
1 tablespoon chopped fresh rosemary
¾ cup grated Parmesan cheese
2 tablespoons unsalted butter, melted
½ cup heavy cream

Preheat the oven to 400°F. Grease a 9-inch round cake pan, line the bottom with a round of parchment paper, and grease the parchment.

Cut the potatoes into ¼-inch-thick slices. Layer the potatoes in the cake pan, overlapping the slices to form an even layer. Sprinkle with the grated onion, salt, black pepper, nutmeg, rosemary, and Parmesan. Finish by pouring the melted butter and heavy cream over the potatoes.

Bake until the potatoes are tender and the cheese is browned, 45 to 55 minutes.

Let cool for 5 minutes. Turn the potatoes out upside down onto a serving dish before slicing into wedges and serving.

Leftover Mashed Potato Pancakes

— **Makes 12 to 14 pancakes** —

In this cookbook, you'll notice a trend of turning leftovers into tasty new meals. Call it whatever you want, but in my family, we've always had a talent for spicing up leftovers. It's not groundbreaking; it's just our way of making the most out of every meal. I think it's a nod to both of my grandmas' cleverness and creativity: they can pretty much take anything and whip up something new. My grandma Alice is a creative wizard in her own right. She's a master at quilting and has made intricate fabric art for most of her life. But when it comes to her food, she'd probably just shrug and say, "I just cook normal food." One of my all-time favorites is when she'd have my sister and me over for lunch. If the electric skillet was out, you knew something awesome was about to happen: mashed potato pancakes. Picture soft, melt-in-your-mouth rounds of pure gold. You can use leftover Party Potatoes (page 121) or any mashed potato recipe you love. While they sit in the refrigerator, they release more starch, holding everything together perfectly. Grandma Alice always threw in some cheese, and after making them myself with and without, it's definitely needed. So, if you decide to whip up these pancakes, I know you'll enjoy each and every bite.

2 cups mashed potatoes
¼ cup all-purpose flour
1 large egg, beaten
½ cup shredded cheddar cheese
1 tablespoon minced fresh thyme
2 tablespoons unsalted butter

Preheat the oven to 200°F.

In a large bowl, combine the mashed potatoes, flour, egg, cheddar, and thyme. Mix to combine.

In a 12-inch skillet or griddle, melt the butter over medium heat. Once the butter is melted, add one scoop (about 2 tablespoons) of the mashed potato batter to the skillet. Press into a small pancake, 2 to 3 inches in diameter. Cook until golden brown, 3 to 4 minutes. Flip the pancakes and repeat. Transfer the cooked pancakes to a baking sheet and keep warm in the oven until they are all finished. Serve hot.

Great-Grandma Hirschy's Egg Noodles with Brown Butter

— Makes 1 pound, serves 6 to 8 —

There's a rich Mennonite heritage woven through every branch of my family tree, with the roots planted firmly both in the Midwest and in the world of farming. From my mom and grandmas to the great-grandmas who came before, they all played a vital role on the farm, helping in their own way by making wholesome meals for their families. For them, recipes were often born from what was on hand, without a strict recipe to guide them. I still find myself smiling at some of my conversations with Grandma Conrad about the dishes her mom used to make. And there's one timeless recipe that stands out: homemade noodles. Great-Grandma was the best at making these noodles, so she made them frequently. My mom, following in her footsteps, would sometimes invite over a friend or two for a noodle-making day. Wooden racks, usually used to dry clothes, were draped with noodles and filled the house until they were ready to be bagged and stored. While we used these noodles in various recipes, my great-grandma kept it super simple: cooked with a brown butter sauce and crowned with toasted bread crumbs. It's a classic that I've kept mostly the same, adding a twist of my own. The butter takes on a toasted, nutty color, infusing the pasta along with a zesty pop of lemon. And to elevate it, a sprinkle of Parmesan cheese makes it even better. This dish truly is a testament to Great-Grandma's wisdom!

FOR THE PASTA
3 large eggs
2 egg yolks
1 tablespoon extra virgin olive oil
2¼ cups all-purpose flour
1 teaspoon kosher salt

FOR THE BREAD CRUMBS
1 tablespoon unsalted butter
1 cup fresh bread crumbs
½ teaspoon kosher salt
1 teaspoon grated lemon zest
½ cup grated Parmesan cheese

TO FINISH
5 tablespoons unsalted butter
½ teaspoon kosher salt
Grated Parmesan cheese, for serving

In a bowl, whisk together the whole eggs, egg yolks, and olive oil.

On the countertop or a large wooden board, mix the flour and salt and make a well in the center of the flour. Add the egg mixture and use a fork to mix the flour into the wet ingredients. Continue to mix until all of the flour is combined with the wet. Knead into a smooth ball. Cover and rest the dough for 30 minutes.

Divide the dough into 4 equal portions. Use a pasta machine or a rolling pin to roll one piece at a time, making sure to flour the dough lightly. Roll anywhere from ⅛ inch to ¼ inch thick. If using a pasta machine, start on setting 1 and roll to setting 4, repeating two times on each setting

(recipe continues)

until getting to the desired thickness. The sheets can be up to 18 to 24 inches long and cut to desired length of noodles.

Once rolled into sheets, cut the noodles into ½-inch-wide strips. The pasta can be dried at this point for longer-term storage.

Prepare the bread crumbs: In a skillet, melt the butter over medium heat. Add the bread crumbs and salt. Stir the bread crumbs until they are toasted and browned, 4 to 6 minutes. Remove from the heat and add the lemon zest and Parmesan. Stir and set aside.

To finish: Bring 4 quarts of water to a boil. Season with salt and add the fresh pasta. Cook until the pasta is tender, 2 to 3 minutes.

In a large skillet, melt the butter over medium heat. Cook the butter until the foaming subsides and it begins to brown and smell nutty, 4 to 6 minutes. Reduce the heat and sprinkle with the salt.

Add the cooked pasta to the brown butter mixture. Toss to coat the noodles. Sprinkle with the bread crumbs and garnish with grated Parmesan cheese. Serve immediately.

Roasted Broccoli & Cauliflower Salad

— Serves 6 —

I came of age at the tail end of the cold salad era; you know, anything from creamy, dressing-laden vegetables to sugary-sweet shredded carrots encased in orange gelatin. Or maybe cold salads were already out of fashion everywhere but the Midwest, and we were simply the last ones to abandon the complex case that is the cold salad. I remember attending church lunches where every lady showcased her prized salad creation, spanning from main courses to desserts. Even Grandma Alice graced our family meals with one or two salads, on top of the traditional lettuce variety. I have a special place in my heart for the iconic broccoli and cauliflower cold salad tossed in a thick mayonnaise dressing. While the flavors of this modernized recipe remain true to that iconic dish, my modern method is totally different, opting for a deconstructed approach with roasted vegetables that are ideally served hot or at room temperature. The result is a slightly lighter yet just as flavorful version, allowing both vegetables to shine in their own right. If you've never experienced the wonder of a cold salad, let this updated recipe be your ticket to savor the charm of my cherished Midwest salad days.

FOR THE ROASTED VEGETABLES
4 cups cauliflower florets
4 cups broccoli florets
2 tablespoons extra virgin olive oil
1 teaspoon kosher salt
1 teaspoon freshly ground black pepper

FOR THE DRESSING
⅓ cup mayonnaise
2 tablespoons full-fat Greek yogurt
2 teaspoons honey
1 tablespoon fresh lemon juice
½ teaspoon kosher salt
¼ teaspoon freshly ground black pepper

FOR THE SALAD
¾ cup dried cranberries
⅓ cup pine nuts

Roast the vegetables: Preheat the oven to 400°F. Line a baking sheet with parchment paper.

Place the cauliflower and broccoli florets on the lined baking sheet. Drizzle with the olive oil, salt, and black pepper. Toss to evenly coat and spread into an even layer.

Roast until they are browned and crisp on the edges, 20 to 25 minutes.

Meanwhile, make the dressing: In a bowl, combine the mayonnaise, Greek yogurt, honey, lemon juice, 1 tablespoon water, the salt, and black pepper. Whisk to combine and add more water as needed for a drizzling consistency. Cover and refrigerate.   *(recipe continues)*

For the salad: When the vegetables are almost finished roasting with 4 to 6 minutes remaining, sprinkle the dried cranberries and the pine nuts on the sheet pan and return to the oven to toast the pine nuts.

Toss everything with the dressing and serve.

Snacks & More

I was initially thinking of labeling this section as appetizers, but it just didn't capture the essence of this mixture of recipes. Yes, many of these gems could totally pass as appetizers, but they're actually all wonderful snack food. These are the munchies that come to the rescue when I need a quick bite or when guests are about to walk through the door, and I need to be armed with something ready to go. In my refrigerator, you'll always find an assortment of quick pickles, which are perfect for that midafternoon crunch (think 2 p.m.) or as the star on a charcuterie board when 7 p.m. hits. Sure, the era of designated appetizer hours may be in the rearview mirror, but snack times are eternal. These recipes are here to keep your taste buds popping and your snack game on point!

Pickle Wrap Puffs

— Makes 24 pieces —

I vividly remember church and family reunion potluck meals holding a plate piled as high as possible with delicious pickle wrap bites. I'll never know who created this genius combination, but it certainly was an appetizer triumph, or so it seemed to me while chowing down on each bite. For those who may not know, a pickle wrap begins with flour tortilla shells that are then generously coated with a luscious cream cheese spread, layered with ham, and finished with a crisp dill pickle on top. Once rolled and sliced, it's a spiral work of art! The marriage of sharp pickles, velvety cream cheese, and savory ham, all wrapped up in a tortilla, made it an instant favorite. While the original version has great flavor, swapping out the tortilla for puff pastry makes it even better. It's a way to take the humble pickle wrap and elevate it to a perfect appetizer or a side snack, with no extra work necessary. The flaky puff pastry encases the trio of cream cheese, pickles, and ham. Baked to perfection, the pastry emerges puffed and golden brown, ready to be sliced into tempting bite-sized morsels or left in larger pieces. For anyone who was never keen on a pickle wrap, this baked recipe promises to wow you with every bite.

4 ounces cream cheese, at room temperature
¼ cup chopped fresh parsley
2 cloves garlic, minced
2 teaspoons Worcestershire sauce
2 teaspoons Dijon mustard
1 sheet frozen puff pastry, thawed
1 cup finely diced dill pickles
6 slices deli ham
1 teaspoon everything bagel seasoning

Preheat the oven to 400°F. Line a baking sheet with parchment paper.

In a bowl, combine the cream cheese, parsley, garlic, Worcestershire sauce, and mustard until the cream cheese is evenly mixed with the ingredients.

On a lightly floured surface, roll the sheet of puff pastry to 10 × 12 inches. With a long side facing you, spread the cream cheese mixture over the pastry, leaving ½ inch empty on the long side farthest from you. Sprinkle with the diced dill pickle and lay the pieces of ham over the top. Starting on the long side nearest you (with the filling to the edge), roll the pastry into a log. Pinch tightly lengthwise to create a seam. Cut into 24 slices and place them on the lined baking sheet. Sprinkle with the everything bagel seasoning.

Bake until the pastry is puffed and browned, 20 to 25 minutes.

Holiday Horseradish Cheese Dip

— Makes 2½ cups —

We were not one of those families steeped in the art of entertaining with cocktail hours and an abundance of fancy appetizers. Our farm life in rural Iowa took a different path. I'm willing to go out on a limb and wager that we never had a single party where a one-bite appetizer was normal. Instead, our version of anything resembling a cocktail hour unfolded during Christmas, when the extended family gathered for what we fondly referred to as "snack time." Truth be told, this really meant dips, relish plates, and the revered pickle plate aplenty. This horseradish cheese dip was a staple during those snack times. The combination of ingredients is unique but culminates in a savory, creamy spread with a subtle kick from the horseradish. While crackers and relishes serve as worthy companions to this dip, imagine it slathered on a grilled cheese sandwich. The options for this recipe are endless, making it the perfect dish for savoring and sharing.

¾ cup evaporated milk
2 cups shredded yellow cheddar cheese
6 ounces cream cheese, at room temperature
1 teaspoon Dijon mustard
½ teaspoon kosher salt
¼ cup prepared horseradish
1 tablespoon hot sauce

In a saucepan, bring the evaporated milk to a simmer over medium heat, 4 to 6 minutes. Reduce the heat to medium-low. Add the cheddar, cream cheese, mustard, salt, horseradish, and hot sauce. Stir until the mixture is smooth, 1 to 2 minutes.

Pour the dip into a serving bowl and refrigerate until chilled and firm, 2 to 4 hours. If desired, drizzle additional hot sauce on top when ready to serve.

Layered Bean Dip

At one time, I viewed the recipes of my upbringing as relics of the past, their place confined to the pages of my childhood and a bit passé today. We're inundated daily with food content. Opening a phone means we will see countless recipes being shown to us in fast motion. Each one claims to be new and interesting and something we need to make. The thing is, I've found that I keep going back to recipes that I know and love from childhood. Yes, some are just begging for a modern twist, while others stand all on their own as timeless classics with cherished memories attached. Layered bean dip, or the classic seven-layer dip, is one of the latter. There are innumerable ways that this crowd-pleaser could be reimagined or updated, but why tamper with perfection? I loved taking this to my church youth group, knowing everyone would dig right in. There's a unique satisfaction in knowing you've brought the most popular appetizer to the party. Layered bean dip has become a staple across much of the United States, not only for its adaptability but more for its mass appeal. While variations abound, the core components remain the same: seasoned refried beans, homemade guacamole, dollops of sour cream, tomatoes in some form, and any number of toppings to finish. In this recipe, I sprinkle pickled peppers and a pairing of cheeses on top. No matter the final touches, this dish makes any party that much better, from the first bite to the last scoop.

One 16-ounce can refried beans
One 4-ounce can diced green chiles
2 cups full-fat Greek yogurt or sour cream
2 tablespoons taco seasoning
2 cups Fresh Guacamole (page 156)
2 cups diced grape tomatoes
2 tablespoons minced onion
3 tablespoons chopped fresh cilantro
1 clove garlic, minced
1 jalapeño, seeded and diced
1 teaspoon kosher salt
½ teaspoon freshly ground black pepper
2 tablespoons lime juice
¾ cup crumbled Cotija cheese
½ cup shredded cheddar cheese
½ cup chopped pickled hot peppers
Chopped scallion

In a bowl, combine the refried beans and green chiles. Mix evenly and spread on the bottom of a 9 × 9-inch baking dish.

In a small bowl, stir together the Greek yogurt and taco seasoning. Spread the mixture over the beans, followed by the guacamole.

In another bowl, combine the tomatoes, onion, cilantro, garlic, jalapeño, salt, black pepper, and lime juice. Stir and allow the mixture to sit for 5 minutes. Drain any collected juice and sprinkle the mixture over the guacamole.

Top with the Cotija, cheddar, pickled peppers, and scallion.

Fundido Taco Cheese Dip

— Serves 4 to 6 —

Informally dubbed "MYF dip" in homage to my church youth group's acronym, this recipe holds a special place in my culinary career. We'd meet once per week, and each youth member, in turn, was tasked with contributing a snack. When it was my turn, I found myself mentally recalculating the time since someone had last brought this dip. Known as a local snack-scene staple, it aptly walked the line between subtly spiced and irresistibly creamy, boasting a texture that's perfect for dipping. I've adapted the original recipe here by introducing a fundido, where the melding of shredded cheese and cream cheese creates a luscious, velvety sauce, eliminating the need for processed cheese. This revamped version, a testament to simplicity, doesn't require a youth group event to enjoy, just a bag of tortilla chips. Any party, whether big or small, will do!

½ **pound fresh chorizo sausage**
½ **onion, diced**
1 **jalapeño, seeded and diced**
4 **ounces cream cheese**
1 **pound Monterey Jack cheese, shredded**

Preheat the oven to 350°F. Line a baking sheet with parchment paper.

In an 8-inch ovenproof skillet, sauté the chorizo, onion, and jalapeño over medium heat until the meat is browned, 6 to 8 minutes. Remove from the heat and drain any excess oil.

Cube the cream cheese into small pieces and mix with the shredded Monterey Jack. Pile the cheese on top of the browned meat. Set the skillet on the lined baking sheet.

Bake until the cheese is melted and bubbling, 10 to 12 minutes. Remove from the oven and serve immediately.

Note: This dip is best served immediately when the cheese is perfectly melted. If it sits too long, it will need to be reheated.

Roasted Veggie Snack Pizza

You may have your own nostalgic memory of vegetable pizza, but it's important to clarify that this isn't your typical hot pizza pie adorned solely with veggies. This appetizer emerged in the '90s, utilizing a can of biscuits to make a crust, slathering it with cream cheese spread, and topping it with raw, chopped vegetables. I always enjoyed it, maybe too much, but I've always felt that there was room for improvement. The raw vegetables sometimes provided a somewhat abrasive texture, and the canned biscuits tended toward blandness. This revamped recipe takes those familiar concepts and makes them even better with a flaky puff pastry and the addition of roasted vegetables. The roasting process maintains a crisp-tender texture to the vegetables, eliminating their raw bite while still leaving a slight crunch. The flavor is elevated even further through the caramelization achieved while roasting, resulting in a terrific update to this iconic childhood classic.

1 sheet frozen puff pastry, thawed
All-purpose flour, for rolling the dough
4 ounces cream cheese, at room temperature
1 tablespoon full-fat Greek yogurt
2 teaspoons whole-grain mustard
2 teaspoons dried dill weed
½ teaspoon garlic powder
½ teaspoon onion powder
1 cup small cauliflower florets
1 cup small broccoli florets
½ cup thinly sliced carrot
½ red bell pepper, thinly sliced
2 scallions, sliced
2 teaspoons extra virgin olive oil
¾ teaspoon kosher salt
¼ teaspoon freshly ground black pepper
2 tablespoons chopped fresh chives
1 tablespoon balsamic glaze

Preheat the oven to 425°F. Line a baking sheet with parchment paper.

Roll the puff pastry out on a lightly floured surface just enough to smooth the seams. Place the pastry on the lined baking sheet. Using a sharp knife, score a perimeter border ½ inch in from the edge, making sure not to cut all the way through the pastry. Place the prepared pastry in the refrigerator to keep cold.

In a bowl, stir together the cream cheese, yogurt, mustard, dill weed, garlic powder, and onion powder until evenly combined. Spread the cream cheese mixture over the prepared pastry, leaving the ½-inch border exposed. *(recipe continues)*

In a bowl, combine the cauliflower, broccoli, carrot, bell pepper, scallion, olive oil, salt, and black pepper. Toss to combine and spread evenly over the cream cheese layer.

Bake the pizza until the crust is golden brown and the vegetables are beginning to brown, 20 to 24 minutes.

Let cool for 5 minutes. Cut into pieces. Sprinkle with the chopped chives and drizzle with the balsamic glaze.

Broiled Cheese Salad Toasts

— Makes 15 to 20 toasts —

I only recently connected the dots that pimento cheese dip, a classic Southern food staple, is pretty much the exact same thing as the spread I used to be obsessed with as a kid. We called it cheese salad, I assume because locally it is in cookbooks under that name, and Grandma Conrad whipped it up every Christmas without fail. We ate this as a dip or in a sandwich when we would congregate at her house for our holiday celebration. Grandma's small yellow Tupperware of cheese salad would be in the refrigerator, ready to be pulled out at snack time. It wasn't just a family thing, though. Back in high school, whenever the cafeteria served chili, you could bet your lunch money they'd also set out a platter of this cheese salad slathered between slices of bread. And it was the highlight of those days. Now, I love to melt it on pieces of bread, like fancy little toasts. It's the kind of thing you can toss together for a chili night or break out when you're feeling a bit fancy and want to be assured that you have an ultimate crowd-pleaser.

FOR THE PIMENTO CHEESE
¾ cup mayonnaise
2 ounces cream cheese, at room temperature
8 ounces yellow cheddar cheese, shredded
2 large hard-boiled eggs, diced
2 tablespoons sweet pickle relish
One 4-ounce jar pimento peppers, drained
½ teaspoon garlic powder
¼ teaspoon onion powder
½ teaspoon kosher salt
½ teaspoon freshly ground black pepper
2 teaspoons hot sauce

FOR THE TOASTS
1 baguette (see Notes), cut into ½-inch slices
Extra virgin olive oil, for drizzling
Kosher salt and freshly ground black pepper

Make the pimento cheese: In a large bowl, stir together the mayonnaise and cream cheese until smooth. Add the cheddar, hard-boiled eggs, pickle relish, pimento peppers, garlic powder, onion powder, salt, black pepper, and hot sauce. Stir together until the mixture is evenly combined.

Assemble the toasts: Preheat the oven to 425°F. Line a baking sheet with parchment paper.

Place the baguette slices on the lined baking sheet. Drizzle with some olive oil and season with salt and black pepper.

Bake until the toasts are beginning to brown on the edges, 6 to 7 minutes. Remove from the oven and set the oven to broil. *(recipe continues)*

Spread 1 tablespoon of the prepared pimento cheese dip on each toast. Place in the oven under the broiler until the cheese is melting and beginning to brown, 6 to 10 minutes.

Remove from the oven and serve immediately.

Notes:

If desired, the pimento cheese can also be served chilled with crackers or used as the filling for a sandwich rather than spreading on the toasts.

A standard grocery store baguette will yield 15 to 20 slices.

Roasted Zucchini, Dill & Feta Dip

— Serves 6 to 8 —

I'll confess: I'm deep into a long-term love affair with dips. Any dip has the power to make my heart sing, but my favorites are hummus, guacamole, and aioli. Honestly, anything that I can dunk my crudités or chips and crackers into is a win in my book. Now, what takes my happiness to the next level is discovering a new way to make use of zucchini from the garden; and this recipe is so good that I've actually found myself buying zucchini from the store in the off-season. The star of the show here is oven-roasted zucchini. Roasting it at a high temperature creates a beautifully browned, almost charred crust on the outside. And remember that color equals flavor. It's then amped up with a mix of tahini, dill, and feta. The end result is a dip that's nothing short of perfection. It's perfect for veggies, pita chips, or even as a spread on a sandwich. How you choose to love it best is entirely up to you!

1 pound zucchini (about 2 medium), trimmed
4 tablespoons extra virgin olive oil
1 teaspoon kosher salt
½ teaspoon freshly ground black pepper
½ cup full-fat Greek yogurt
⅓ cup tahini
2 cloves garlic
2 ounces feta cheese, plus more for garnish
2 tablespoons chopped fresh dill, plus more for garnish
2 tablespoons fresh lemon juice

Preheat the oven to 425°F. Line a baking sheet with parchment paper.

Slice the zucchini lengthwise into ¼-inch-thick planks. Place the zucchini on the lined baking sheet. Drizzle with 2 tablespoons of the olive oil and sprinkle with the salt and black pepper.

Roast until the zucchini is well browned, 20 to 25 minutes.

Transfer the roasted zucchini to a blender or food processor. Add the remaining 2 tablespoons olive oil, the Greek yogurt, tahini, garlic, feta, dill, and lemon juice. Blend until the mixture is smooth, about 1 minute. If the dip is thick, add water 1 tablespoon at a time to achieve a dipping consistency.

Pour into a bowl and garnish with fresh dill and more feta cheese.

Fresh Guacamole

— Serves 6 to 8 —

Guacamole wasn't a traditional part of my childhood foods repertoire. Our Sunday night routine included post-church chips with melted cheese and home-canned salsa, but there was never an avocado in sight. The guacamole revelation happened during high school at my friend Megan's house, thanks to her mom, Monica, who was often whipping up huge (and I truly mean huge) batches of this dip. The creamy avocados paired with the zing of lime juice created a flavor sensation I didn't know I was missing but desperately needed in my life. While I've tried innumerable store-bought versions, none have compared to the superior taste of homemade guacamole. Crafting it in your own kitchen ensures you nail the texture to your liking. After some fiddling over the years, I've landed on the perfect recipe, realizing that simplicity is the secret, with the right balance of acid to salt. This is the ultimate "you'll never need to buy it again" super-fresh guacamole recipe that's satisfying.

5 or 6 avocados
1 teaspoon kosher salt
2 tablespoons fresh lemon juice
¼ cup lime juice
1 jalapeño, seeded and diced
¼ cup chopped fresh cilantro
2 cloves garlic, minced
½ cup diced red onion

Halve and pit the avocados. Scoop the flesh into a large bowl. Add the salt, lemon juice, lime juice, jalapeño, cilantro, garlic, and onion. Use a fork to mash the mixture together until it reaches the desired texture.

Spiced Nuts, Three Ways

My earliest memory of spiced nuts involves irresistible, craggy pecans dusted with a generous coating of sugar and a bit of cinnamon. I've always loved to snack on nuts, mostly in their raw form, but these were something magical. It all started when we received a batch of sugared nuts as a holiday gift. My sister re-created them pretty much the next day with her own mixture of pecans, sugar, and cinnamon stirred together, resulting in the most delightful treat. That simple yet wonderful combination inspired my recipe for crunchy sugared pecans, encompassing all of the textures and flavors that had me hooked from the start. This can all be made in a skillet and truly is a terrific gift to give during the holiday season. My world of spiced nuts expanded beyond sugar later in life when I began to entertain in my own home and wanted something simple sitting on the counter or as part of a snack plate ready when friends arrived, so I developed two savory mixed-nut recipes. My recipe for sweet and smoky nuts has a hint of sweetness and warm, savory spices. It truly makes any party better. The herb and olive oil nuts boast a richness from chopped fresh herbs tossed with olive oil, creating a delicious blend of flavors. These spiced and sugared nuts have become a staple in my arsenal when I need something quick and easy that will always be a hit. Do not fall prey to thinking special nuts are just for holiday use; make these year-round.

Crunchy Sugared Pecans

— Makes 4 cups —

1 egg white
¾ cup sugar
4 cups pecans
2 teaspoons ground cinnamon
½ teaspoon ground allspice
¼ teaspoon ground cloves
1 teaspoon kosher salt
1 teaspoon vanilla extract

Preheat the oven to 350°F. Line a baking sheet with parchment paper.

In a large bowl, whisk the egg white and sugar until it is frothy, about 2 minutes.

Add the pecans, cinnamon, allspice, cloves, salt, and vanilla and stir to combine. Pour onto the lined baking sheet and spread into an even layer.

Bake until they are crunchy, 18 to 22 minutes.

Let cool before serving.

Sweet & Smoky Nuts

— Makes 3 cups —

3 cups unsalted roasted mixed nuts

3 tablespoons light brown sugar

3 tablespoons maple syrup

2 tablespoons orange juice

2 teaspoons smoked paprika

½ teaspoon garlic powder

¼ teaspoon cayenne pepper

1 teaspoon kosher salt

1 tablespoon minced fresh thyme

Preheat the oven to 350°F. Line a baking sheet with parchment paper.

In a large bowl, stir together the mixed nuts, brown sugar, maple syrup, orange juice, smoked paprika, garlic powder, cayenne, salt, and thyme. Pour onto the lined baking sheet and spread into an even layer.

Roast, stirring halfway through, until they are glazed, 18 to 20 minutes.

Let cool for 20 minutes before breaking into pieces and serving.

Herb & Olive Oil Nuts

— Makes 3 cups —

3 cups unsalted roasted mixed nuts

2 tablespoons extra virgin olive oil

1 tablespoon maple syrup

2 teaspoons minced fresh rosemary

2 teaspoons fresh thyme leaves

1 teaspoon garlic powder

1 teaspoon kosher salt

½ teaspoon freshly ground black pepper

Preheat the oven to 350°F. Line a baking sheet with parchment paper.

In a large bowl, stir together the mixed nuts, olive oil, maple syrup, rosemary, thyme, garlic powder, salt, and black pepper. Pour onto the lined baking sheet and spread into an even layer.

Roast, stirring once, until the nuts are toasted and dry, 16 to 20 minutes.

Let cool for 10 minutes before serving.

Quick Pickles

My family has an unwavering love for pretty much any type of pickle—a love that has been nurtured through years of canning and preserving. Grandma Conrad had a passion for pickling and would meticulously tweak her classic recipes each year. Whether she was reducing the salt by half a teaspoon or introducing a couple of garlic cloves, every adjustment was aimed at perfection, even if the changes seemed minute. When I'd stop by her house, she would pull out an assortment of jars and ask me for my thoughts. Some of the changes were so nuanced that I couldn't detect a difference, but Grandma was adamant about her pursuit of perfection. To this day, I still can a lot of pickles each summer, but I also make quicker versions when needed. These pickle recipes are similar to Grandma's refrigerator pickles, and all represent versions of the pickles I preserve each year. Utilizing a strong brine, the fresh vegetables are quickly infused with flavor, eliminating the need for the water-bath

canning process, which is welcome news to many who find canning to be a difficult art to master. Once stored in the refrigerator, they're ready for eating in a matter of hours. But the benefits of a refrigerator pickle are more than just their quick preparation time. The vegetables retain their crisp texture since they don't go through a water-bath cooking process, and the flavors are vibrant and pungent. What's even better is that the recipes can easily be adapted with any number of spices. Whether one or all of these quick pickle variations find a permanent place in your refrigerator, I hope they become a staple in your home soon, too!

Quick-Pickled Cucumbers

— Makes 1 quart —

1 cup distilled white vinegar
1 tablespoon kosher salt
1 tablespoon sugar
¾ teaspoon dill seeds
1 teaspoon peppercorns
1 teaspoon mustard seeds
1 pound cucumbers
1 sprig fresh dill

In a small saucepan, combine the vinegar, 1 cup water, the salt, sugar, dill seeds, peppercorns, and mustard seeds. Bring the brine to a simmer over medium heat and whisk until the salt and sugar are dissolved, 2 to 3 minutes. Remove from the heat and set the brine aside to cool slightly.

Slice the cucumber into ¼-inch-thick slices or spears. Place the cucumber in a clean 1-quart jar or two pint jars along with the fresh dill. Pour the cooled brine over the cucumbers.

Cover with a lid and refrigerate for at least 24 hours before eating.

Quick-Pickled Carrots

— **Makes 1 quart** —

1 pound carrots
4 sprigs fresh thyme
1 cup apple cider vinegar
1 tablespoon kosher salt
1 tablespoon sugar
1 teaspoon cumin seeds
1½ teaspoons chipotle powder
2 cloves garlic, smashed

Peel and cut the carrots into sticks. Place the sticks and sprigs of thyme into a 1-quart jar or two pint jars.

In a small saucepan, combine the vinegar, 1 cup water, the salt, sugar, cumin seeds, chipotle powder, and garlic cloves. Bring the brine to a simmer over medium heat and whisk until the salt and sugar are dissolved, 2 to 3 minutes.

Pour the hot brine over the prepared carrots. Allow the brine to cool to room temperature.

Cover with a lid and refrigerate for at least 24 hours before eating.

Quick-Pickled Green Beans

— Makes 1 quart —

1 pound green beans, trimmed
⅓ cup sliced onion
1 cup distilled white vinegar
1 tablespoon kosher salt
1 tablespoon sugar
1 teaspoon dill seeds
¼ teaspoon red pepper flakes (optional)

Place the beans and onion into a 1-quart jar or two pint jars.

In a small saucepan, combine the vinegar, 1 cup water, the salt, sugar, dill seeds, and pepper flakes. Bring the brine to simmer over medium heat and whisk until the salt and sugar are dissolved, 2 to 3 minutes.

Pour the hot brine over the prepared green beans and onions. Allow the brine to cool to room temperature.

Cover with a lid and refrigerate for at least 24 hours before eating.

Quick-Pickled Giardiniera

— Makes 1 quart —

2 red chiles, sliced in half

1 red bell pepper, diced

1 rib celery, cut into ¼-inch pieces

2 carrots, cut into ¼-inch pieces

1 small head cauliflower, cut into
   bite-sized florets

2 cloves garlic, smashed

1 cup distilled white vinegar

1 tablespoon kosher salt

2 teaspoons sugar

2 teaspoons dried oregano

1 teaspoon red pepper flakes

1 teaspoon black peppercorns

In a large bowl, combine the red chiles, bell pepper, celery, carrots, cauliflower, and garlic and toss to combine. Pack the mixture into a 1-quart jar or two pint jars.

In a saucepan, combine the vinegar, 1 cup water, the salt, sugar, oregano, pepper flakes, and peppercorns. Bring the mixture to a simmer over medium heat and simmer until the sugar and salt are dissolved, 2 to 3 minutes.

Pour the hot brine over the prepared vegetables. Allow the brine to cool to room temperature.

Cover with a lid and refrigerate for at least 24 hours before serving.

Sweet Corn Day

As a kid, Sweet Corn Day held the title as my ultimate summer ritual. Both of my grandmas would be there, along with Grandpa and sometimes my cousins, all gathered to prepare sweet corn for the freezer so we could enjoy it year-round. In the thick humidity of August in Iowa, Grandpa and Dad would wake up before the sun to handpick the ears of corn. Once ready, we formed an assembly line under the big silver maple in the east yard, where we shucked each ear by hand. Grandma Alice, the designated silk-checker, ensured everyone's were silk-free. It was a crucial step before the sweet corn made its way to the kitchen. There, we cooked it immediately followed by a quick chill. Grandma Conrad verified that each ear was chilled to the core before skillfully cutting off the kernels. Now, some people may swear by cutting off the raw corn, but in our family, those are fighting words. We stand by the old-school method: cook, chill, and then cut off.

Nowadays, the tradition has evolved a bit, with Mom, my stepdad, and me taking up the torch (albeit with a more manageable number than the 200+ pints we use to do), the spirit remains intact. When my sister and her family join in during the harvest, the kitchen once again buzzes with the energy and chaos I fondly recall from my childhood. It's all about too many people in the kitchen, echoing laughter, and the sweet aroma of freshly prepared corn filling the air. Some traditions, no matter how they change with the generations, always manage to create special moments.

Salads

I'm a firm believer in the appeal of salads, and I'll always be a champion for them. On many nights, instead of a full meal, I fill a bowl with greens, top it with roasted vegetables, and drizzle it with a delicious dressing. That's the beauty of a salad: it can be whatever you want it to be. When it comes to my favorite salads in this section, I approached them with a mindset of evolution. The flavors and ingredients may have a familiar ring, but I've given them a modern twist, transforming them into something I would crave every day. The untossed salad (see page 180) is one where I've taken the most freedom, and now it has become my go-to craving, a combination of flavors and textures in every bite. Then there's the Honey Dijon Three-Bean Salad (page 190), with the flavors just as I remember, but with fresh green beans and an amped-up dressing to bring a sharper kick. These recipes aren't your grandma's salads; they're modern go-tos crafted to make you fall in love with salads all over again.

Untossed but Tossed Salad

— Serves 4 to 6 —

When I picture my favorite salad growing up, I think about how out of place it seems in today's vibrant salad scene filled with fresh greens and inventive dressings. Our family's "untossed salad," commonly known as a seven-layer salad, feels like a relic these days. Traditionally, we began with a base of crisp iceberg lettuce, followed by layers of diced onion, peas, hard-boiled eggs, chopped bacon, and Swiss cheese, all topped off with a generous slathering of mayonnaise. This was a particular favorite of my dad's, and I wholeheartedly shared in his love for it. While I still indulge in our traditional version occasionally, the copious amount of mayonnaise and the lack of overall flavor make it less suitable for an everyday salad. In this reimagined version, I've transformed the recipe into a salad worthy of any day of the week. I kick things off with high-quality romaine lettuce and layer on all the components from the original: bacon, hard-boiled eggs, and peas. The addition of goat cheese levels up the salad with a more complex flavor profile. The key component, though, is the homemade buttermilk ranch dressing. Departing from the singular, heavy flavor of traditional mayonnaise, this dressing bursts with the freshness of multiple herbs. Now it's a salad I enjoy as often as I want, seamlessly taking the place of the original without sacrificing any of my treasured nostalgia.

FOR THE SEED-NUT CLUSTERS
1 tablespoon unsalted butter
1 tablespoon honey
½ cup Marcona almonds, chopped
¼ cup sunflower seeds
2 tablespoons sesame seeds
½ teaspoon garlic powder
⅛ teaspoon cayenne pepper
¼ teaspoon kosher salt
¼ teaspoon freshly ground black pepper

FOR THE SALAD
1 large head romaine lettuce or 2 smaller romaine hearts, chopped
2 cups baby arugula
Buttermilk Ranch Dressing (recipe follows)
2 cups peas
1½ cups chopped cooked bacon
4 large hard-boiled eggs, diced
4 ounces goat cheese

Make the seed-nut clusters: In a small skillet, melt the butter and honey over medium heat. Add the Marcona almonds, sunflower seeds, sesame seeds, garlic powder, cayenne, salt, and black pepper. Stir and toast the mixture until the almonds are beginning to lightly brown, 4 to 6 minutes. Remove from the heat and pour the mixture onto parchment paper to cool.

Assemble the salad: On a large platter or bowl, toss the lettuce and arugula with some of the dressing.

Add the peas, bacon, hard-boiled eggs, and goat cheese. Add more dressing as needed and top with the cooled seed and nut mixture.

(recipe continues)

Buttermilk Ranch Dressing

— Makes ¾ cup —

¼ cup mayonnaise
¼ cup buttermilk
2 tablespoons full-fat Greek yogurt
1 tablespoon fresh lemon juice
2 tablespoons chopped fresh dill
1 tablespoon chopped fresh parsley
1 tablespoon chopped fresh basil
1 tablespoon minced shallot
1 clove garlic, minced
¼ teaspoon kosher salt
¼ teaspoon freshly ground black pepper

In a bowl, combine the mayonnaise, buttermilk, yogurt, lemon juice, dill, parsley, basil, shallot, garlic, salt, and black pepper. Using an immersion blender or countertop blender, blend until smooth with some small pieces of herbs still intact. Store in an airtight container in the refrigerator for up to 1 week.

Weeknight Taco Salad

Taco salad is my ultimate rescue meal, my secret weapon in times of need. There is something so satisfying about having a meal you can pull out of your back pocket whenever life throws something unexpected at you. I have my mom to thank for this. Come summer, we'd usually be out in the garden, working until the sun went down. Exhausted but hungry, Mom's taco salad would come to the rescue. Cooking up some seasoned meat takes mere minutes. Throw in beans and lettuce, and our late-night summer dinner was good to go. Over the years, I've tweaked my own taco salad recipe to become something I absolutely love. Rather than ground beef, I've switched things up and used ground chicken instead. It's lean, and I love how it soaks up all of the spices. And to swap out the tortilla chips, I've introduced some necessary crunch with toasted cooked quinoa. Trust me; it's a game-changer: packed with protein and oven-crisped for the perfect crunchy topping. Back in the day, we never bothered with a fancy dressing for our taco salad. It was simply whatever type of dressing was in the refrigerator. But my jalapeño lime dressing takes this salad to an entirely new level. It's the secret sauce that transforms a good meal into a well-rounded, perfect one. Cheers to taco salad for being the rescue meal we all need!

FOR THE CRISPY QUINOA

2 cups cooked quinoa (cooked according to package directions)

3 tablespoons neutral oil

1 teaspoon kosher salt

2 teaspoons taco seasoning

2 teaspoons lime juice

FOR THE CHICKEN & BEANS

1 tablespoon neutral oil

1 onion, diced

2 cloves garlic, minced

1 pound ground chicken

1 teaspoon kosher salt

1 tablespoon taco seasoning

1 teaspoon ground cumin

¼ teaspoon cayenne pepper

One 15-ounce can kidney beans, drained and rinsed

FOR THE SALAD

1 large head romaine lettuce or 2 romaine hearts, chopped

2 cups shredded red cabbage

Jalapeño Lime Dressing (recipe follows)

1 cup sweet corn kernels freshly cooked, frozen, or canned

1 cup sliced cherry tomatoes

Grated Cotija or shredded cheese, for garnish

Crushed tortilla chips, for garnish

Cilantro, for garnish

Preheat the oven to 375°F. Line a baking sheet with parchment paper.

Make the crispy quinoa: In a bowl, toss the quinoa with the oil, salt, taco seasoning, and lime juice. Spread evenly onto the baking sheet.

(recipe continues)

Bake, stirring every 15 minutes, until the quinoa is crisp and toasted, 45 to 55 minutes. Set it aside to cool.

Meanwhile, prepare the chicken and beans: In a large skillet, heat the oil over medium heat. Add the onion and sauté until softened and beginning to brown, 4 to 6 minutes. Stir in the garlic and cook until fragrant, about 30 seconds.

Add the ground chicken, break it into small pieces, and stir until it is fully cooked, 6 to 8 minutes. Add the salt, taco seasoning, cumin, and cayenne pepper. Stir and add the kidney beans. Remove from the heat and set aside.

Assemble the salad: On a large platter or bowl, toss the lettuce and red cabbage with some of the jalapeño lime dressing. Add the chicken/bean mixture, crispy quinoa, sweet corn, and cherry tomatoes. Top with more dressing and garnish with cheese and tortilla chips.

Jalapeño Lime Dressing

— Makes ¾ cup —

¼ cup lime juice
2 tablespoons full-fat Greek yogurt
2 teaspoons agave syrup or honey
2 teaspoons Dijon mustard
2 cloves garlic, minced
1 jalapeño, seeded
½ teaspoon kosher salt
⅓ cup neutral oil
1 cup roughly chopped fresh cilantro

In a countertop blender, combine the lime juice, yogurt, agave, mustard, garlic, jalapeño, salt, oil, and cilantro. Blend until smooth with small pieces of cilantro remaining. (Alternatively, use an immersion blender.) Store in an airtight container in the refrigerator for up to 1 week.

Summertime Coleslaw

— Serves 4 to 6 —

If there was a competition for the hardest-working salad dressing out there, this one would undoubtedly be in the running. While I don't anticipate jaws on the floor after tasting this for the first time, I do expect a new group of cooks to keep this in their refrigerator at all times. For years, my usage of this dressing was confined to shredded cabbage for coleslaw, but that was a total underestimation of its potential, as it's pretty much delicious on anything. This recipe began with the advent of blenders. As new kitchen appliances hit the market, companies published recipe pamphlets to demonstrate their various uses, and this was surely how my family's recipe was born. While this particular dressing has endured the passage of time, I've fine-tuned it over the years. Instead of copious amounts of sugar, my version includes just enough honey to balance the acidity. An onion not only contributes to the flavor but, when blended, serves as a natural emulsifier, transforming the dressing into a creamy delight without the need for any dairy. The outcome is a combination of bold flavors and a light texture, reminiscent of a vinaigrette. This, for me, is the quintessential coleslaw dressing, so say goodbye to the mayonnaise-dominated versions and get ready for the arrival of a new, albeit authentically old, kid in town.

Notes:

I like a mixture of red and green cabbage for this salad.

Store any leftover dressing in the refrigerator.

FOR THE BLENDER COLESLAW DRESSING

¾ cup neutral oil
⅓ cup apple cider vinegar
1 teaspoon celery seeds
2 teaspoons Dijon mustard
1 teaspoon kosher salt
½ teaspoon freshly ground black pepper
2 tablespoons honey
¾ cup roughly chopped white onion

FOR THE NUT TOPPING

2 teaspoons extra virgin olive oil
1 teaspoon honey
¼ cup sunflower seeds
¼ cup slivered almonds
¼ teaspoon garlic powder
¼ teaspoon kosher salt
¼ teaspoon freshly ground black pepper

FOR THE SLAW

1 pound cabbage (see Note), shredded
1 carrot, shredded

Make the blender coleslaw dressing: In a blender, combine the neutral oil, vinegar, celery seeds, mustard, salt, black pepper, honey, and onion. Blend the dressing until it is smooth. (Alternatively, do this with an immersion blender.)

Make the nut topping: In a small skillet, combine the olive oil, honey, sunflower seeds, slivered almonds, garlic powder, salt, and black pepper. Stir the mixture over medium heat until it is toasted and glazed, 4 to 6 minutes. Remove from the heat and pour the mixture onto parchment paper to cool.

Assemble the slaw: In a large bowl, combine the shredded cabbage and carrot. Toss with dressing to taste. Add the nut topping and serve.

Spring Garden Lettuce Salad

This recipe serves as proof that creating a stellar salad doesn't require a lengthy list of ingredients or intricate techniques. Both of my grandmothers would pull out this recipe each spring, taking advantage of the tender, freshly harvested lettuce from the garden. The salad itself was a minimalist combination of crisp, garden-grown lettuce, a bit of onion, and a distinctive dressing. This time-honored dressing, made from a blend of mayonnaise, vinegar, sugar, and seasonings, was a staple in kitchens across the Midwest. When the lettuce was ready to be picked, this dressing could be quickly whisked together, transforming an ordinary vegetable into a delicious side dish. In today's world, not everyone has access to fresh garden lettuce, but if you want to give gardening a try, lettuce is an excellent starting point. Rather than follow my grandmas' recipe to the letter, I personally enjoy tossing in shallots for a subtly softer flavor. As for the dressing, if time allows, making homemade mayonnaise will be far superior to anything store-bought. A touch of apple cider vinegar and honey is all that's needed to achieve a perfectly balanced dressing. Enjoying this salad during the spring season is an excellent reminder of the skill possessed by my grandmothers and countless others, showcasing their ability to create exceptional dishes with only a handful of ingredients.

½ cup mayonnaise, preferably homemade (page 80)
2 tablespoons apple cider vinegar
2 teaspoons honey
½ teaspoon kosher salt
½ teaspoon freshly ground black pepper
2 heads Buttercrunch lettuce or fresh garden lettuce, torn into pieces
1 shallot, sliced
Homemade Croutons (recipe follows)

In a small bowl, whisk together the mayonnaise, vinegar, honey, salt, and black pepper until smooth.

In a large bowl, toss the lettuce and shallot with the desired amount of dressing and top with croutons. This is best served fresh, as the dressing will wilt the tender leaves of the lettuce over time.

Homemade Croutons

4 cups cubed bread, sliced into ½-inch cubes
2 tablespoons extra virgin olive oil
2 tablespoons unsalted butter, melted
1 teaspoon onion power
1 teaspoon garlic powder
½ teaspoon kosher salt
½ teaspoon freshly ground black pepper

Preheat the oven to 350°F. Line a baking sheet with parchment paper.

In a large bowl, add the cubed bread, olive oil, melted butter, onion powder, garlic powder, salt, and black pepper, and toss until everything is well-combined.

Spread evenly on the baking sheet and bake for 12 to 18 minutes until golden and slightly crisp. Store any leftover croutons in an airtight container for 1 week.

Honey Dijon Three-Bean Salad

— Serves 4 to 6 —

When most people see a recipe with the word "salad" in the title, a certain image is conjured in the imagination. My goal is to dispel the idea that a salad must always contain lettuce. And there are so many options for ingredients that steer away from the mundane and everyday. A personal favorite of mine is the classic three-bean salad, a mixture of kidney beans, wax beans, and green beans. In the traditional recipe, the dressing tended to be overly sweet and lacking in actual flavor. With just a few tweaks, this recipe can emerge as a satisfying departure from the norm. Instead of using canned green beans, which are limp and flavorless, I opt for fresh ones, blanching them to preserve their crisp texture and robust flavor. In lieu of wax beans, I love to add chickpeas, which strike a delightful balance between their soft interior and firm exterior. The dressing takes a Dijon-forward approach, resulting in a vibrant vinaigrette. When the beans are mixed into this mustardy and acidic dressing, it not only breaks through the starch but also blends the flavors. Trust me, this revamped version is ready to become a cherished family favorite in your home.

Kosher salt
1 pound fresh green beans, trimmed
1 clove garlic, minced
1 tablespoon Dijon mustard
2 teaspoons honey
½ teaspoon freshly ground black pepper
2 tablespoons white wine vinegar
4 tablespoons extra virgin olive oil
One 15-ounce can red kidney beans, drained and rinsed
One 15-ounce can chickpeas, drained and rinsed
½ red onion, sliced

Set up a large bowl of ice water and have it near the stove. Bring 3 quarts of water to a boil. Add 1 tablespoon salt and the green beans. Boil for 2 minutes. Remove the beans from the water and plunge them into the prepared ice water. Stir the beans until they are fully chilled, about 6 minutes. Drain the beans and set them aside to dry.

In a small bowl, whisk together the garlic, mustard, honey, ½ teaspoon salt, the black pepper, vinegar, and olive oil. Whisk until the vinegar and oil are emulsified. Set the dressing aside.

Cut the green beans into thirds and place them in a bowl. Add the kidney beans, chickpeas, and red onion. Pour on the dressing, toss, and serve.

Fresh Cucumber Salad

— Serves 4 to 6 —

Cucumber salad didn't appear on my culinary radar until middle school, a surprising fact considering my mom's love of pickles. While she can't resist pickles, she hates fresh cucumbers. This is ironic, especially during our pickle-making times when she occasionally has to hold her nose to get through the raw cucumber scent. Only after the pickles have sat long enough to lose their raw taste does she dive into them wholeheartedly. Unfortunately, this aversion meant cucumber salad never made an appearance on our table at home. Thankfully, one day while visiting Grandma Conrad's, she mentioned whipping up a batch, and my ears perked up. I was hooked by its simplicity, almost like a quick pickle but with less of a vinegar-y touch. Since then, I've played with the recipe, making it my own. The secret weapon is fresh dill. Unlike the strong taste of the dill seeds used in pickles, fresh dill fronds add a lighter, more nuanced flavor to this dish. The dressing used to toss the cucumbers is a straightforward vinaigrette, enhancing without overpowering the crispness of the cucumbers. I've made this a summer staple in my house, keeping a batch in the refrigerator all season long. All credit goes to Grandma Conrad and that fortuitous encounter at her home.

¼ cup rice vinegar
¾ teaspoon kosher salt
1 teaspoon sugar
½ teaspoon freshly ground black pepper
2 tablespoons chopped fresh dill
⅓ cup extra virgin olive oil
½ red onion, sliced
2 hothouse cucumbers (about 1½ pounds), sliced

In a bowl, combine the vinegar, salt, sugar, black pepper, dill, and olive oil. Whisk to dissolve the sugar and salt. Add the sliced onion and cucumbers. Stir to coat the onion and cucumber in the dressing. Cover and marinate for 20 minutes before serving.

Spinach Salad with Lentils & Apples

— Serves 4 to 6 —

I'm really into growing spinach for a couple of reasons. First, I just hands down love to eat it. And second, it's one of the first things I plant in my spring garden, which means I'm usually inundated with it for quite a while. After a long winter, March hits, and as soon as the snow melts, I'm usually out in the garden beds planting seeds, maybe pushing my luck a bit before it's officially recommended. Before the heat of summer and dry weather force me to supplement with water in the garden, spinach proliferates without any extra help, making it a super-easy green. But, after planting a few rows, I end up with spinach overload. So, it has become my ongoing mission to use it all up without letting any go to waste. Spinach finds its way into any number of my cooked dishes, and I make sure to blanch and freeze some for later. But the first thing I always do is prepare a massive spinach salad. I grew up on a traditional version of spinach salad, with radishes, hard-boiled eggs, and bacon. It was the real taste of spring. I still make that one, but my taste buds have shifted, instead craving a salad that brings a bit more brightness, heartiness, and some new textures to the table. Here, the lentils soak up the bright vinaigrette, giving them a starchy protein goodness. A crisp crunch comes in from the apple and toasted walnuts, while dried cranberries add a sweet, soft note. And the feta cheese adds that perfect briny finish that ties it all together. I call it my spring salad, but truth be told, I gobble it up all the way into fall. Give it a shot, and I think you'll do the same!

FOR THE RED WINE VINAIGRETTE

1 tablespoon minced shallot

1 clove garlic, minced

1 tablespoon Dijon mustard

1 teaspoon whole-grain mustard

½ teaspoon kosher salt

¼ teaspoon freshly ground black pepper

2 tablespoons red wine vinegar

1 tablespoon orange juice

2 teaspoons maple syrup

½ cup extra virgin olive oil

FOR THE SALAD

5 ounces spinach, washed, long stems removed

1 orange, segmented

1 crisp apple, thinly sliced

1 cup cooked lentils

1 cup toasted walnuts, roughly chopped

¾ cup dried cranberries

½ cup crumbled feta cheese

Make the red wine vinaigrette: In a bowl, combine the shallot, garlic, Dijon mustard, whole-grain mustard, salt, black pepper, vinegar, orange juice, maple syrup, and olive oil. Whisk until the oil is emulsified with the vinegar.

Assemble the salad: In a large bowl, arrange the spinach. Top with the orange segments, apple, and lentils. Toss with some of the vinaigrette.

Top with the toasted walnuts, dried cranberries, and feta. Drizzle with more dressing to taste and serve.

Desserts

Get ready for a celebration of desserts that cater to every skill level and sweet tooth. My mantra in this section is that every recipe is a breeze, but some just like to take their sweet time. Believe it or not, even if you've never donned an apron, baking a perfect Roasted Strawberry Rhubarb Pie (page 241) is totally doable. And for those moments when time is of the essence, my Raspberry Oat Crumb Bars (page 227) are the ultimate quick fix. These desserts aren't just for special occasions; they're freezer-friendly delights ready to steal the show at a moment's notice. If you grew up in the Midwest, you know how to work a freezer for long-term dessert storage, especially cookies. And here's a little secret: if you think desserts aren't your thing, one bite of these goodies will change your mind. Let's dive into some of my favorite desserts and whip up some treats!

Apple Snack Cake

— Serves 9 to 12 —

During the dewy days of spring and the warm evenings of summer, I find myself caught up in everything to do with my garden, spending most of my day working on my unending checklist until the sun sets. Baking rarely crosses my mind during these times, as the idea of warming up the house with the oven seems crazy. With the arrival of September, though, a subtle dip in the temperature lets me know that it's about time to shift indoors. Walking through our orchard and seeing a few apples scattered on the ground gives me the urge to bake. I'll admit that it often takes me by surprise as the summer always seems to fly by, but I won't lie that I truly anticipate the coziness of indoor time. The first thing on my fall baking list is this apple snack cake. There's no need for heavy equipment, as everything can easily be mixed by hand. I find it relaxing to peel apples in the kitchen, perhaps with a new fall-scented candle burning, and embrace the promise of the new season. This cake's moistness comes from the inclusion of applesauce, which is often used in place of oil for those wanting less fat. I love the subtle flavor it adds to the apples, giving them a secret little boost, all from the same fruit. Unlike traditional frosted cakes, this recipe has a cinnamon sugar crust that I can't describe any other way than perfection. So, whether it's a new season or you just need to feel cozy, this is the cake to bake!

Nonstick baking spray
8 tablespoons unsalted butter, at room temperature
½ cup granulated sugar
½ cup packed light brown sugar
1 large egg
1 cup unsweetened applesauce
2 cups all-purpose flour
1 teaspoon baking soda
¼ teaspoon baking powder
¾ teaspoon kosher salt
½ teaspoon ground allspice
½ teaspoon ground cinnamon
2½ cups diced peeled apples

FOR THE CINNAMON SUGAR TOPPING
1 tablespoon granulated sugar
½ teaspoon ground cinnamon

Preheat the oven to 350°F. Grease a 9 × 9-inch baking dish.

In a large bowl, cream the butter and both sugars until they are light and fluffy, about 3 minutes. Add the egg and mix until it is evenly combined. Scrape the sides and bottom of the bowl. Add the applesauce and mix, 1 to 2 minutes. The batter will look broken, which is normal.

Add the flour, baking soda, baking powder, salt, allspice, and cinnamon. Fold the apples into the batter. Pour the batter into the prepared baking dish.

Make the cinnamon sugar topping: In a small bowl, combine the sugar and cinnamon. Sprinkle the cinnamon sugar over the batter.

Bake until the cake is golden brown and a skewer inserted in the middle comes out clean, 40 to 50 minutes. Let cool for 30 minutes before slicing.

One-Layer Birthday Cake

—— **Serves 6 to 8** ——

Growing up in rural Iowa, almost all my relatives lived within a few miles of our farm. So, it's no surprise that when it came to birthday celebrations, it was easy for everyone to be together. My sister and I had birthdays three days apart, so our birthdays naturally occurred as a joint party. When you're young, you think everything in your world is normal, so none of this felt that special. Nowadays, my sister and her family live all the way across the country in Virginia, so getting together at the drop of a hat is not possible. But today, remembering the importance of those family get-togethers, I've made it a goal to celebrate the birthdays of my two nieces and nephew with a cake. Over the years, I've baked large, multitiered cakes with lots of leftovers to store in the freezer. Then it hit me to make this simple one-layer cake. It's easy, full of buttery flavor, and perfect for a celebration or a weeknight snack. The whipped buttercream frosting creates a smooth, fluffy topping that delivers the perfect finish to a perfect cake.

FOR THE CAKE
Nonstick baking spray
10 tablespoons unsalted butter, at room temperature
¾ cup granulated sugar
1 large egg
2 egg yolks
¾ cup buttermilk
1 teaspoon vanilla extract
1 cup all-purpose flour
1¼ teaspoons baking powder
½ teaspoon kosher salt

FOR THE FROSTING
8 tablespoons unsalted butter, at room temperature
2 ounces dark chocolate, melted and cooled
¼ cup Dutch-process cocoa powder, sifted
¼ cup heavy cream
1 teaspoon vanilla extract
1 cup powdered sugar, sifted
¼ teaspoon kosher salt

Preheat the oven to 350°F. Grease an 8-inch or 9-inch round cake pan and line the bottom with a round of parchment paper.

In a stand mixer, cream together the butter and granulated sugar until they are light and fluffy, 3 to 5 minutes. Add the whole egg and egg yolks one by one, incorporating well before adding the next. Scrape the sides of the bowl.

In a separate bowl, stir together the buttermilk and vanilla. In a third bowl, combine the flour, baking powder, and salt. With the mixer on low speed, add one-third of the flour mixture, followed by half of the buttermilk mixture.

(recipe continues)

Repeat the additions, ending with the final one-third of flour. Mix until the flour mixture is just incorporated.

Remove the bowl from the mixer and fold by hand to ensure everything is evenly mixed. Pour into the prepared baking pan and smooth out to evenly fill the pan.

Bake until a skewer inserted into the middle comes out clean, 27 to 30 minutes.

Let cool for 10 minutes in the pan before turning out onto a wire rack to cool completely.

Make the frosting: In a stand mixer, combine the butter, melted chocolate, cocoa, heavy cream, vanilla, powdered sugar, and salt. Beat on low to incorporate the ingredients. Turn the speed up to medium and beat until it is smooth.

Frost the cooled cake and serve.

Grandma's Special-Occasion Cream Puffs

— Makes 16 cream puffs —

When we're children, we don't realize that the magic of the holidays needs to be created by the adults in our lives. Every facet, from the special menu to the festive decorations and carefully curated guest list, is thoughtful and considered. My grandma Alice was the self-selected orchestrator of the magic of our family's special occasions. We'd make the short trip across the road to Grandma and Grandpa's farm, ready for a full meal for eleven, my aunt and uncle and cousins included. Alone, she'd make all of the magic happen, with everything seemingly appearing without any effort. One thing she often did was add something special to the meal. Sometimes, it was an appetizer at each plate or a special dessert. Her recipe for these cream puffs was one of the special desserts I loved the most. I now understand that cream puffs are pâte à choux, a quick pastry that magically puffs in the oven, creating a cavity within the puff that can be filled. At the time, they seemed like the most amazing dessert that only Grandma Alice could bake. She'd often serve these with ice cream in the middle and maybe even a drizzle of chocolate sauce. These special touches made the memories, which is why I love them all the more.

FOR THE CHOUX PASTRY
8 tablespoons unsalted butter
½ cup whole milk
2 tablespoons sugar
½ teaspoon kosher salt
1 cup all-purpose flour
4 large eggs
Egg wash: 1 egg, beaten

TO FINISH
4 ounces dark chocolate, chopped into small pieces
½ cup plus 2 tablespoons heavy cream
1 tablespoon unsalted butter
Vanilla ice cream

Position racks in the top and bottom thirds of the oven and preheat the oven to 400°F. Line two baking sheets with parchment paper.

Make the choux pastry: In a 4-quart saucepan, combine the butter, ½ cup water, the milk, sugar, and salt. Set the pan over medium heat, whisk to combine, and bring to a boil. Once boiling, add the flour all at once. Whisk constantly until the mixture forms a paste, 1 to 2 minutes. Continue to cook until the paste forms a film on the bottom of the pan, 3 to 4 minutes.

Remove from the heat and, using a stand mixer, whisk in one egg at a time, fully incorporating before adding the next one. The batter should be smooth and silky. Pour the batter into a pastry bag or a large zip-top bag.

Cut a ½-inch opening in the pastry bag and pipe sixteen 2-inch-wide mounds of batter on the lined baking sheets. Dip a finger in water and

(recipe continues)

smooth the point at the top of the pastry. Brush each puff with egg wash.

Bake for 15 minutes. Reduce the oven temperature to 350°F and bake until the cream puffs are golden brown, about 20 minutes.

Remove from the oven and cool on the pan.

To finish: Put the chocolate in a glass bowl. In a small saucepan, heat the cream until it is steaming and immediately pour it over the chopped chocolate. Cover and allow the

chocolate to melt, about 5 minutes. Stir until the ganache is smooth. Add the butter and stir until it is melted.

To serve, slice a cream puff in half, creating a lid and a base. Add a scoop of ice cream to the bottom half of the cream puff and place the lid on top. Drizzle with the warm ganache and serve. If the ganache cools and is firm, heat in the microwave in 10-second increments until it easily pours.

Cardamom & Orange Zucchini Loaf Cake

— Serves 8 to 10 —

Come summer, ask any seasoned gardener, and they'll entertain you with tales of the zucchini struggle: the endless fluctuation between an abundance and scarcity of zucchini. To be honest, it's the curse of growing this vegetable. In those lucky years when the vines thrive and evade the vine borers, my harvest is nothing short of a zucchini overload. I harvest them both morning and evening and always seem to find a forgotten one that grew ten sizes too big and has boat-like proportions. The following year, if I'm a bit more lax in terms of the insects, I may have zucchini plants that appear robust until they quickly meet their demise. For this reason, I never complain about having too many zucchini. Instead, I work to find all the ways to use it! While zucchini bread bears the nomenclature of "bread," it's really a cake in the guise of bread. Enter the zucchini loaf cake, a dessert that is acceptable at any hour, thanks to its bread-like slices. This particular recipe stands as my forever favorite, because it is moist and infused with the vibrant notes of orange zest and cardamom, offering a nice change from the conventional. A reduction in the amount of sugar as compared to many older zucchini bread recipes makes slices of this cake pair wonderfully with a pat of butter or a scoop of ice cream.

Nonstick baking spray
2 large eggs
½ cup full-fat Greek yogurt
¼ cup neutral oil
¾ cup granulated sugar
1 teaspoon vanilla extract
1 tablespoon grated orange zest
2 cups all-purpose flour
1 teaspoon baking powder
1 teaspoon baking soda
½ teaspoon kosher salt
½ teaspoon ground allspice
½ teaspoon ground cardamom
2 cups grated zucchini
1 tablespoon turbinado or granulated sugar

Preheat the oven to 350°F. Grease one 8½ x 4½-inch loaf pan, or two smaller loaf pans.

In a large bowl, whisk the eggs until they are smooth. Whisk in the Greek yogurt, oil, granulated sugar, vanilla, and orange zest to evenly incorporate.

In a separate bowl, mix together the flour, baking powder, baking soda, salt, allspice, and cardamom. Add the flour mixture to the wet ingredients and fold until partially incorporated. Add the grated zucchini and fold in until everything is fully incorporated. Pour into the greased loaf pan(s) and sprinkle with the turbinado sugar.

Bake until the bread is golden brown and a skewer inserted in the middle comes out clean, 50 to 60 minutes for the loaf pan, 25 to 35 minutes for smaller pans.

Let cool in the pan for 20 minutes, then turn out onto a wire rack to cool completely.

Sort-of-Homemade Ice Cream Dessert

— Serves 12 to 15 —

My love for ice cream is earned honestly. It was one of those things we always had in our freezer, no matter the time of year. Like Dad always said, ice cream works to fill in all of the cracks, even after a hearty meal. My sister and I weren't allowed to have it daily, but I vividly remember not being able to sleep one night, groggily going downstairs, only to find Dad eating ice cream. I think this was a nightly occurrence for him, but you can understand the audacity and betrayal I felt. My innocent mind struggled to comprehend that adults could simply eat ice cream whenever they chose! Fast-forward to the present, and I now do the same, keeping ice cream in my freezer at all times. You, too, may discover me standing in my kitchen late at night eating ice cream, just like my dad. Ice cream is an easy dessert on its own but just as easy to make into a special treat. This recipe is a quick one that can be made ahead, stored in the freezer, cut into squares, and served. It tastes like it took time, but no one needs to know the secret that it doesn't. Serve this for a birthday party, after a summer meal, or stand in your kitchen late at night eating it straight from the pan. You and I will keep that secret together.

4 cups crispy rice cereal
⅓ cup packed light brown sugar
½ teaspoon ground cinnamon
1 cup unsweetened shredded coconut
1 cup chopped pecans
¼ teaspoon kosher salt
12 tablespoons unsalted butter, melted
½ gallon vanilla ice cream

FOR THE CARAMEL SAUCE
2 tablespoons light corn syrup
1 cup granulated sugar
1 cup heavy cream
3 tablespoons unsalted butter
½ teaspoon vanilla extract
¼ teaspoon kosher salt

Preheat the oven to 300°F.

In a large bowl, combine the rice cereal, brown sugar, cinnamon, coconut, pecans, and salt. Using hands, partially crush the cereal and mix the ingredients together. Add the melted butter and mix to incorporate evenly. Pour half of the crumbs into a 9 × 13-inch baking dish. Press firmly into a crust. Pour the remaining crumbs onto a baking sheet and spread into an even layer.

Bake both the baking sheet and baking dish until the crumbs are toasted, 20 to 25 minutes. Set aside to cool.

Once cooled, allow the vanilla ice cream to soften slightly. Scoop the ice cream over the bottom crust and smooth it into an even layer. Top with the toasted crumbs. Cover and freeze until the ice cream is firm, 4 to 6 hours.

(recipe continues)

Desserts

Make the caramel sauce: In a saucepan, stir together ¼ cup water, the corn syrup, and granulated sugar. Set over medium heat and, without stirring more, allow the water to come to a boil. Continue to cook, swirling the pan as needed for even cooking, until the sugar is golden and turns to caramel, 8 to 12 minutes.

Remove from the heat and slowly whisk in the cream. It will bubble vigorously. Add the butter, vanilla, and salt and stir until smooth. Let the caramel sauce cool slightly.

Once the ice cream is firm, slice into pieces and serve with warm caramel sauce drizzled on top.

Butterscotch Pudding with Meringue Topping

For years, the perfect recipe for homemade butterscotch pudding eluded me. This is my favorite flavor, but one we had never made at home. We made pudding often in our kitchen, especially when milk teetered on the brink of spoiling. My mom was keen on minimizing waste, so she'd quickly whip up the typical vanilla and chocolate puddings. Making pudding itself is a straightforward endeavor, but the complexity of butterscotch flavor, like what we've all become accustomed to with store-bought alternatives, means that it isn't easy to mimic at home. Years ago, I talked to Grandma Conrad about this, and she got a twinkle in her eye. She had the perfect method to create a deeply flavored butterscotch pudding, starting with the gentle burning of sugar. Sugar melts at high heat and eventually darkens, creating the true essence of butterscotch. The addition of dark brown sugar further deepens these flavors, resulting in a smooth and creamy masterpiece. Grandma had an eye for a bit of decadence and preferred to adorn the top of her butterscotch pudding with a crown of meringue. It's a tradition I've wholeheartedly embraced. You don't need to wait for your milk to be on the verge of spoiling to make this pudding. In fact, I recommend not waiting at all!

FOR THE PUDDING
¾ cup packed dark brown sugar
½ cup all-purpose flour
1 teaspoon kosher salt
1½ cups whole milk
4 egg yolks
¼ cup granulated sugar
1⅓ cups heavy cream
3 tablespoons unsalted butter
1½ teaspoons vanilla extract

FOR THE MERINGUE
4 egg whites
1 cup granulated sugar
¼ teaspoon kosher salt
1 teaspoon vanilla extract

Make the pudding: In a medium bowl, mix together the dark brown sugar, flour, and salt. Add the milk and egg yolks and whisk until it is smooth. Set aside.

In a small saucepan, heat the cream until it is steaming. Set aside.

Pour the granulated sugar into a 4-quart saucepan and shake the pan so the sugar is in an even layer. Set it over medium heat. Do not stir, but watch closely. When the sugar begins to turn clear and becomes a liquid, slowly swirl the pan until it is all melted, 6 to 8 minutes. Continue to cook the sugar until it is a dark amber color, 4 to 6 minutes.

Remove the sugar from the heat and slowly add the warm cream. The sugar will bubble, and some will solidify. Return the saucepan to medium heat

(recipe continues)

Desserts

and stir until the sugar has melted into the cream, 4 to 6 minutes.

Remove the mixture from the heat and while whisking, slowly pour the hot cream/sugar mixture into the egg yolk/milk mixture to temper the yolks. Return the mixture to the saucepan.

Set the pan over medium heat and whisk constantly until it becomes thick with large bubbles forming in the middle of the pudding, 6 to 8 minutes. Remove from the heat.

Add the butter and vanilla and stir until smooth. Pour into a 10-inch pie plate. Cover with plastic wrap, pressing the wrap directly onto the surface of the pudding to prevent a skin from forming. Refrigerate the pudding for 1 hour or up to 2 days.

When ready to serve, make the meringue: In the bowl of a stand mixer, combine the egg whites, granulated sugar, and salt. Whisk until smooth, then set the bowl over a pan of barely simmering water on the stove. Whisk the mixture until the sugar is dissolved and it reaches 160°F, 6 to 8 minutes. Remove from the heat.

Snap the whisk onto the stand mixer and whisk on medium speed for 1 minute. Add the vanilla, increase the speed to medium-high, and whisk until it is white with thick, stiff peaks, about 7 minutes.

Spread the meringue frosting over the pudding. It can be browned under a broiler or served immediately.

Blackberry Biscuit Cobbler

— Serves 9 —

A cobbler is one of the best quick fruit desserts. There's no fussing around with rolling out dough, no stressing about crimping edges, and definitely no guessing game as to when it's perfectly baked. This dessert is all about simplicity with minimal ingredients: a hint of sugar, some thickener, and a squeeze of lemon juice to amp up that fruit flavor. Mix it all up, pour it into a baking dish . . . and that's where the dessert debates usually kick in. What really sets a cobbler apart from a crisp or a brown betty? Well, I'm sidestepping that entire argument and declaring a drop biscuit topping as the champion. A drop biscuit is made from wet dough with spoonfuls dropped generously over the fruit filling. They work their magic in the oven, turning golden, puffing up, and becoming a sugary crisp crust on top, warm on their underside by blackberries. (Any berry works, but let's give blackberries the spotlight for once.) Trust me on this one; try this drop biscuit–topped blackberry magic, and you'll never go back to any other cobbler recipe again.

Nonstick baking spray

FOR THE BLACKBERRY FILLING
6 cups blackberries
¼ cup sugar
2 tablespoons cornstarch
1 tablespoon fresh lemon juice
1½ teaspoons vanilla extract

FOR THE DROP BISCUITS
1½ cups all-purpose flour
1½ teaspoons baking powder
¼ teaspoon baking soda
5 tablespoons sugar
½ teaspoon kosher salt
6 tablespoons cold unsalted butter,
    cut into ½-inch pieces
1 large egg
½ cup buttermilk

Preheat the oven to 350°F. Grease a 9 × 9-inch baking dish.

Make the blackberry filling: In a large bowl, combine the blackberries, sugar, cornstarch, lemon juice, and vanilla. Stir together to dissolve the cornstarch and pour into the prepared baking dish.

Make the drop biscuits: In a large bowl, mix together the flour, baking powder, baking soda, 4 tablespoons of the sugar, and the salt. Add the cubed butter and toss to coat in the dry mixture. Work the butter into the flour by pressing pieces of butter between thumb and forefinger until all the butter is worked in with no pieces bigger than a pea. *(recipe continues)*

In a small bowl, whisk together the egg and buttermilk until smooth. Pour it into the dry mixture and stir together to form a shaggy, wet, and cohesive mass. Use a scoop to make 9 equal biscuits on top of the blackberry filling. Sprinkle the top of the biscuits with the remaining 1 tablespoon sugar.

Bake until the filling is bubbling in the center and the biscuits are golden brown, 45 to 55 minutes.

Let cool for 1 hour before serving.

Rhubarb Custard Pie Bars

— Serves 12 —

Before I knew better, rhubarb never struck me as anything special. Everyone I knew in Iowa had a large patch in their backyard. Most of the time, it was there way before the current homeowners even moved in, just doing its thing year after year without anyone giving it a second thought. That's the beauty of rhubarb; it's a perennial vegetable that returns yearly with very little fuss. I didn't realize how lucky we were to have rhubarb on demand until I grew up and found out not everyone has a rhubarb bed in their yard. Imagine my shock when I discovered people actually had to pay for it at the farmers' market or grocery store. So, if you've got a sunny spot in your yard, here's my pitch for you to start growing rhubarb. Plant it now, watch it grow, and know that there's very little work to be done. Plus, it's one of the first things you can grab from your garden every year. Most people think of rhubarb as a dessert ingredient, and I'm not here to change that idea. Rhubarb has a sour, bright flavor, but it plays so well with sugar. I always anticipate the first stalks of ripe rhubarb so I can bake these pie bars: a combination of a buttery shortbread crust and a creamy custard layer dotted with pieces of rhubarb. It's basically a giant slab pie, but even better.

Nonstick baking spray

FOR THE CRUST
1½ cups all-purpose flour
¾ cup powdered sugar
¼ teaspoon kosher salt
12 tablespoons cold unsalted butter

FOR THE FILLING
4 large eggs
1½ cups granulated sugar
1 teaspoon grated orange zest
½ cup all-purpose flour
¼ cup heavy cream
1 teaspoon vanilla extract
¼ teaspoon kosher salt
4 cups chopped rhubarb

Preheat the oven to 350°F. Grease a 9 × 13-inch baking dish.

Make the crust: In a large bowl, mix together the flour, powdered sugar, and salt. Cube the butter into ½-inch pieces and add the cubes to the dry ingredients. Toss the pieces of butter to coat them in the dry mixture. Using thumbs and forefingers or a pastry cutter, work the butter into the mixture until it is crumbly and resembles wet sand.

Spread and press the mixture evenly into the prepared pan, forming the crust.

Bake the crust until it is set and beginning to brown around the edges, 12 to 15 minutes.

Meanwhile, make the filling: In a large bowl, whisk the eggs until they are smooth. Add the granulated sugar and whisk until it is pale yellow

(recipe continues)

and frothy, 2 to 3 minutes. Add the orange zest, cream, vanilla, flour, and salt and whisk the custard until smooth.

Remove from the crust from the oven and while it is still warm, sprinkle the chopped rhubarb evenly over the crust. Pour the custard over the rhubarb and return the bars back to the oven.

Bake until the top is browned, the edges are set, and the center slightly jiggles, 37 to 40 minutes.

Let cool for 1 hour before slicing and serving.

Refrigerator Oatmeal Cookies

— Makes 28 to 32 cookies —

Refrigerator cookies were like the original slice-and-bake before you could just buy premade cookie dough at the grocery store. Back in the day, before the ease of cookies in a tube, Grandma had an entire book of recipes for just this type of cookie. You whip up the dough, roll it into a log, and put it in the refrigerator or freezer for future use. When the craving hits, just slice and bake. And let me tell you, these cookies are legitimately one of Grandma's best recipes. Refrigerator cookies have a higher ratio of butter when compared to traditional drop cookies, resulting in a tender, buttery cookie similar to a sablé cookie. My bet is that this cookie will become one of your family favorites, especially with the luscious smooth frosting spread on top. But fair warning: you might not be able to resist the urge to bake them right after mixing them together. They're almost too tempting to resist.

FOR THE COOKIES

16 tablespoons unsalted butter, at room temperature
½ cup granulated sugar
½ cup packed light brown sugar
1 large egg
1 teaspoon vanilla extract
2 cups all-purpose flour
1½ cups quick-cooking oats
¼ cup malted milk powder
½ teaspoon baking soda
¾ teaspoon kosher salt

FOR THE FROSTING

3 tablespoons unsalted butter, at room temperature
4 tablespoons heavy cream
1 teaspoon vanilla extract
⅛ teaspoon kosher salt
1½ cups powdered sugar, sifted

Make the cookies: In a stand mixer, combine the butter and both sugars. Beat until well incorporated and light, 3 to 5 minutes. Add the egg and vanilla and beat to incorporate. Scrape the sides of the bowl.

Add the flour, quick oats, malted milk powder, baking soda, and salt. Mix until no dry streaks of flour remain. Divide the dough onto two pieces of parchment paper and form each into an 8-inch log. Wrap tightly and chill until firm, 3 to 4 hours.

Once firm, preheat the oven to 350°F. Line baking sheets with parchment paper.

Slice ½-inch-thick cookies and place them on the lined baking sheets. *(recipe continues)*

Bake until they are lightly browned, 10 to 12 minutes.

Let the cookies cool on the pan for 5 minutes before transferring to a wire rack to cool to warm.

Make the frosting: In a bowl, combine the butter, cream, vanilla, salt, and powdered sugar. Whisk until smooth.

Frost each slightly warm cookie with ½ teaspoon frosting and return to the rack until the glaze is hardened.

Macerated Strawberries with Sweet Cornmeal Biscuits

— Serves 8 —

Of all the tasks that you could have heard me complaining about when I was young, it was never the chore of picking strawberries. Ask my mom, and she might tell a different story. I was raised with the idea that if you love eating something, you'd better lend a hand in growing it. We had two large strawberry beds in the garden—one on the east end, the other on the west. As they grow, the plants shoot out runners that spawn new plants. We'd let them stretch out in one direction, starting new plants, while pulling out some old ones to keep the berries young and boost production. The beds shifted back and forth over time as they matured. In case you haven't had the pleasure of experiencing strawberry season, it's a super-quick thing. Since we loved growing June-bearing berries, it lasted a few short weeks in June, just like the name suggests. But once we had a bucket full of strawberries, the first thing we did, and I still do, was slice and macerate the berries. Sometimes, we'd simply heap them on vanilla ice cream, but if we were lucky, they'd be spooned on top of shortcakes. This recipe takes shortcakes to a whole new level by adding cornmeal for a touch of sweetness and texture. It may seem small, but it truly is a game changer. This is my unbeatable go-to for shortcakes—a seasonal treat that's worth the wait all year until strawberry season swings back around.

2 cups all-purpose flour
½ cup yellow cornmeal
5 tablespoons sugar
1 tablespoon baking powder
½ teaspoon baking soda
½ teaspoon kosher salt
8 tablespoons unsalted butter
1¼ cups buttermilk
2 tablespoons melted butter
2 pounds strawberries, hulled and quartered
2 teaspoons limoncello or fresh lemon juice
Whipped cream or ice cream for serving

Preheat the oven to 450°F. Line a baking sheet with parchment paper.

In a large bowl, stir together 1¾ cups of the flour, the cornmeal, 4 tablespoons of the sugar, the baking powder, baking soda, and salt. Cut the cold butter into ½-inch cubes and toss the butter with the dry ingredients to coat all the pieces of butter. Using hands or a pastry cutter, cut in the butter until the pieces of butter are irregular, creating a sandy texture.

Pour in the buttermilk and stir to form a rough, shaggy dough. Dust a work surface with the remaining ¼ cup flour. Dump the dough onto the surface and use the flour to knead the rough dough into a cohesive shaggy mass.

Pat the dough to a rough 12 × 8-inch rectangle. With the long side facing you, cut the dough into thirds and place them on top of each other. Pat out the dough into a 10 × 8-inch rectangle. Repeat this step one more time. On the final time,

(recipe continues)

Desserts

223

roll the dough into a rectangle about ¾ inch thick. Cut six 2½-inch round biscuits and place them on the lined baking sheet. Gather the scraps and roll it out to ¾ inch thick. Cut out 2 more biscuits.

Brush the tops of the biscuits with the melted butter and bake until they have risen and are golden brown, 14 to 16 minutes.

Remove from the oven and brush again with the melted butter.

In a bowl, combine the strawberries, the remaining tablespoon sugar, and the limoncello. Stir until the sugar begins to dissolve. Let the strawberries macerate for 20 minutes before serving.

To serve, slice a biscuit in half lengthwise. Spoon the macerated strawberries over the bottom half. Place the top half face down on the strawberries and serve with a dollop of whipped cream or ice cream.

Raspberry Oat Crumb Bars

— Makes 9 bars —

Years ago, I used to throw together a bake sale every once in a while. There was something so exciting about whipping up treats and seeing what people went crazy for. Maybe it felt natural to me because my mom had done the same thing years earlier, having one every week for a solid decade. She'd dive into days of nonstop baking leading up to Friday morning, getting everything ready beforehand. It was a lot of work, but I think it did wonders for keeping her mind focused and occupied, especially after Dad passed away. Life throws curveballs, and sometimes we just need those moments that give us a sense of purpose and a reason to power through the tough times. I'd tag along with her at times, and after laying out all the treats on the table, we'd sit and chat with some coffee in hand, conversing with customers as they picked out their favorites. The best part was observing what got people excited and kept them coming back week after week. When it came time for my own bake sale, these raspberry oat bars were always the bestseller. The crust and topping are like a soft, chewy granola bar, and the filling is packed with raspberry flavor with a perfect sweet-tart balance. You don't need a bake sale to see that you'll be whipping up these bars each week. They're just that good.

Nonstick baking spray
1¼ cups all-purpose flour
1¼ cups rolled oats
¾ cup packed light brown sugar
½ teaspoon kosher salt
½ teaspoon baking soda
1½ teaspoons ground cinnamon
12 tablespoons unsalted butter
1 cup raspberry preserves
¾ cup raspberries, fresh or frozen

Preheat the oven to 350°F. Grease an 8 × 8-inch baking dish and line it with parchment paper with two sides overhanging (to make a sling). Grease the parchment.

In a large bowl, combine the flour, oats, brown sugar, salt, baking soda, and cinnamon. Mix together. Add pieces of butter and work into the dry ingredients using hands or a pastry cutter. Squeeze the butter and dry mixture between fingers until the mixture becomes like wet sand with pieces of butter the size of peas or smaller.

Pour 2 cups of the crumb mixture into the prepared baking dish. Lightly press to form an even crust. Place the crust in the oven and bake for 10 minutes. Remove from the oven to cool slightly, about 10 minutes. Leave the oven on.

Spread the raspberry preserves over the crust. Sprinkle with the raspberries and top with the remaining crumb mixture.

Bake until the top turns slightly browned and puffed in the middle, 30 to 35 minutes.

Let cool for at least 4 hours before cutting into 9 squares.

Pumpkin Pie Cake

— **Makes 9 squares** —

This pumpkin pie cake recipe might not reinvent the wheel, but there's a reason it's a crowd-pleaser. If you haven't tasted this dessert before, picture a rich layer of pumpkin pie topped with a thick, indulgent cake layer. How could that pairing not be everyone's favorite? Traditionally, people relied on a box of cake mix to put this recipe together, but I wanted to kick it up a notch without sacrificing any flavor. No hate to box mix lovers. I get that sometimes things need to be fast and easy to make. I simply like the satisfaction of whipping up something entirely from scratch. And I also think this shows how easy it is to mimic a box with ingredients in our pantries. The pie and cake layers are so incredibly good: thicker, more decadent, and studded with big, craggy pieces of cake. You can slice it up as bars or amp it up with a dollop of whipped cream. It might even be better than traditional pumpkin pie. I know, a bold claim, but once you try it, I'm betting you'll agree.

Nonstick baking spray

FOR THE PUMPKIN LAYER
4 large eggs
⅔ cup heavy cream
One 15-ounce can pumpkin puree
¾ cup sugar
½ teaspoon vanilla extract
½ teaspoon kosher salt
1 teaspoon ground cinnamon
½ teaspoon ground ginger
⅛ teaspoon ground cloves

FOR THE CAKE CRUMB LAYER
2 cups all-purpose flour
1 cup sugar
1½ teaspoons baking powder
½ teaspoon baking soda
½ teaspoon kosher salt
10 tablespoons unsalted butter, melted
2 teaspoons vanilla extract

Preheat the oven to 350°F. Grease a 9 × 9-inch baking dish.

Make the pumpkin layer: In a large bowl, whisk the eggs until they are smooth. Add the heavy cream, pumpkin puree, sugar, vanilla, salt, cinnamon, ginger, and cloves. Whisk to combine and pour into the prepared baking dish.

Make the cake crumb layer: In a medium bowl, stir together the flour, sugar, baking powder, baking soda, and salt. Add the melted butter and vanilla and stir until the dry mixture is moistened and looks like wet sand. Sprinkle the crumb mixture over the filling.

Bake until the cake crumb is golden brown and puffed, 35 to 40 minutes. Let cool fully, 4 to 6 hours. Cut into 9 squares to serve.

Old-Fashioned Brownies

— Serves 9 to 12 —

I have a friend who swears by box-mix brownies. I get it: they have their time and place. But let me try to persuade you that homemade is better. And to prove my point, you only need to try this recipe to know I'm right. All of the ingredients are the usual pantry staples, so there's no need for a grocery store run; you can whip these brownies up on a whim. And what you get is chocolate magic: a rich, gooey brownie with an irresistible shiny, crackly crust on top. Now, when it comes to baking time, that's where the real secret lies. If you love your brownie to be fudgy goodness, stick to the lower end of the suggested time. If you're someone who loves a bit more of a cake-like texture, go for the longer bake time. Just know that when that chocolate smell begins wafting from the oven, it's a sign that the flavor is beginning to leave. So, I usually go for the shorter bake time to lock in all that chocolate goodness. Trust me, once you've had a taste of these homemade brownies, that box mix will be a distant memory. It's time to upgrade your brownie game and say goodbye to the boxed stuff forever.

Nonstick baking spray
8 tablespoons unsalted butter, at room temperature
1 cup granulated sugar
½ cup packed light brown sugar
2 large eggs
2 teaspoons vanilla extract
¾ cup all-purpose flour
½ cup Dutch-process cocoa powder, sifted
½ teaspoon kosher salt
1 cup semisweet chocolate chips

Preheat the oven to 350°F. Grease an 8 × 8-inch baking dish and line it with parchment paper overhanging two sides (to make a sling). Grease the parchment.

In a stand mixer, combine the butter, granulated sugar, and brown sugar and beat until light and fluffy, 3 to 5 minutes. Scrape the sides of the bowl and beat in the eggs one at a time until they are incorporated. Mix in the vanilla.

Add the flour, cocoa powder, and salt and mix until no dry streaks of flour remain, 1 to 2 minutes. Fold in the chocolate chips by hand and pour the batter into the prepared baking dish.

Bake until the brownies are set around the edges and a skewer inserted in the middle comes out mostly clean, 30 to 40 minutes.

Let cool in the pan for 30 minutes before removing and slicing.

Peach Shortcake Bars

— Makes 9 squares —

In a world where we've grown accustomed to having all sorts of fruits available year-round at our grocery stores, there's something beautifully different about peaches. You won't find them out of season, and personally, I love it that way. Anticipation builds up throughout the year, and when those peaches are finally ripe, it's a season worth celebrating. My own peach trees are usually ready to harvest around late July or even into August, but sometimes, you can find peaches in markets a bit earlier. What makes peaches so tricky is that they must ripen on the tree to unlock their full flavor and sweetness. That's precisely why you won't spot them in the grocery store twelve months of the year. It's a bit of a waiting game, but trust me, it's worth it. So, when peaches are ready, you must savor them in every way possible, whether it's eating them as is, baking them into any number of recipes, or, my personal favorite, whipping up these heavenly shortcake bars. This is a simple shortcake dough that acts as both a bottom crust and crumble topping, hugging a hefty layer of fresh peaches. The peaches maintain their fresh summer essence, and when wrapped in the buttery embrace of the bar, they're nothing short of perfection. Peaches stand as a season-based treat, reminding us to savor the moment and savor every bite. These shortcake bars are just the reminder you need!

Softened butter, for the baking dish
16 tablespoons unsalted butter, at room temperature
1 cup granulated sugar
2 egg yolks
1 teaspoon vanilla extract
¼ teaspoon almond extract
2⅓ cups all-purpose flour
1 teaspoon baking powder
½ teaspoon kosher salt
½ cup apricot preserves
2 cups sliced peaches, fresh or frozen
1 tablespoon light brown sugar
1 teaspoon ground cinnamon
½ teaspoon ground ginger

Preheat the oven to 350°F. Line an 8 × 8-inch baking dish with parchment paper overhanging two sides (to make a sling) and butter the exposed sides.

In a stand mixer, cream the butter and granulated sugar until light and fluffy, 3 to 5 minutes. Add the egg yolks one at a time, mixing well after each addition until incorporated. Add the vanilla and almond extract and mix. The dough may look curdled, but that is normal.

Add the flour, baking powder, and salt. Mix until just combined and no dry streaks remain, 1 to 2 minutes. Add half of the dough to the prepared pan and press evenly to create the bottom crust.

Spread the preserves on the bottom crust. Line the sliced peaches over the preserves and overlap the peaches if necessary. Sprinkle with the brown sugar, cinnamon, and ground ginger.

(recipe continues)

Top with the remaining dough by breaking it into irregular pieces evenly over the peaches.

Bake until it is golden on the top and the edges are bubbling slightly from the preserves, 35 to 45 minutes. If the top seems to be getting too brown during baking, cover it with foil.

Let cool completely in the pan, 2 to 4 hours. Cut it into squares to serve.

Crispy-Topped S'Mores Bars

—— **Serves 9 to 12** ——

I'm all for giving classic recipes a modern spin, and these bars hold a special spot in my heart, especially during harvest season on the farm. My mom whipped them up for quick field meals, a simple chocolate cake layer topped with a graham cracker crust. Throw some marshmallows on top, let them get gooey in the oven, and you're halfway there. The final topping includes a mix of chocolate, peanut butter, and crispy rice cereal. These s'mores are unique enough for company and simple enough for a regular weeknight treat. No farming skills are required, just an appetite for a satisfying snack.

Softened butter, for the baking dish
7 whole graham cracker sheets
8 tablespoons unsalted butter
¾ cup sugar
2 large eggs
1 teaspoon vanilla extract
2 tablespoons Dutch-process cocoa powder, sifted
¼ teaspoon baking powder
¾ cup all-purpose flour
2½ cups small marshmallows
¾ cup semisweet chocolate chips
¾ cup creamy peanut butter
1½ cups crispy rice cereal

Preheat the oven to 350°F. Butter a 9 × 9-inch baking dish. Fit the graham crackers into the bottom of the baking dish in a single layer, breaking some as necessary.

In a bowl, cream the butter and sugar together until they are light and fluffy, 3 to 5 minutes. Add the eggs one at a time, beating well until they are incorporated. Mix in the vanilla.

Add the sifted cocoa, baking powder, and flour. Fold the dry ingredients into the wet until they are combined. Pour the batter over the graham crackers in the prepared baking dish.

Bake until the cake is set, 13 to 15 minutes.

Remove the cake from the oven and sprinkle the marshmallows on top. Return the cake to the oven for 3 to 4 minutes to slightly melt the marshmallows. Once the marshmallows have baked and melted into each other, remove the pan from the oven and set it aside to cool.

(recipe continues)

Desserts

In a medium microwave-safe bowl, combine the chocolate chips and peanut butter. Microwave in 30-second increments, stirring after each, to melt the mixture until it is smooth. (Alternatively, set the bowl over a pan of simmering water, making sure the bottom of the bowl doesn't touch the water.)

Fold in the crispy rice cereal and pour it over the marshmallows and cake. Spread to an even layer. Set the cake in the refrigerator to cool for 20 minutes before slicing and serving.

All-Butter Pie Dough

— Makes enough for one 9-inch pie —

As the name suggests, this recipe harnesses the power of butter to create the perfect all-butter pie dough. While butter might not seem like a groundbreaking choice, our family's pie crust recipe never included it. Mom preferred a crust that relied solely on lard, with vinegar and water. The result was decent but lacked flavor—sorry, Mom. After years of experimentation, trying various pie-making techniques, I've decided the all-butter crust is the hands-down winner. Lard and shortening, common ingredients in pie crust recipes, can deliver flakiness, but butter pulls double duty by bringing both flavor and flakiness to the table. The beauty of this dough lies in its versatility, as it can be transformed into anything, be it savory or sweet: tarts, hand pies, galettes, or the classic pie. My mission with this recipe is to empower anyone to confidently whip up a pie. To be honest, not many of us have the luxury of baking pies weekly and storing them in a dedicated pie cabinet like farmers from yesteryear. Instead, we reserve pie-making for special occasions and want the end result to be completely worth the effort. I promise you that this recipe is worth it! The crust becomes an integral part of the finished pie, rather than simply a vessel for the filling. And in case you're wondering, Mom's on board now, too. She's made the switch to this all-butter treat.

1½ cups all-purpose flour
2 tablespoons sugar
1 teaspoon kosher salt
10 tablespoons unsalted butter, cubed
4 to 6 tablespoons ice-cold water

In a large bowl, combine the flour, sugar, and salt. Add the cubed butter and toss with the dry mixture to coat all of the pieces of butter. Using thumbs and forefingers or a pastry cutter, press pieces of butter into the flour. Work the butter into the flour until the pieces of butter are irregular and no larger than a pea.

Add 4 tablespoons of the cold water and toss to combine. The weather and temperature can impact how much water is needed. Pick up a fist of the dough and squeeze. If the dough is crumbly and easily crumbles away, add more water, 1 tablespoon at a time, until it holds together.

Press the dough into an even disk and wrap it tightly. Smooth the edges and refrigerate for 20 minutes. Once chilled, roll out for your desired recipe.

Roasted Strawberry Rhubarb Pie

— Serves 7 to 8 —

If you were to ask me about my favorite pie, I'd give you a different answer each time, driven mainly by the seasons and my ever-changing cravings. However, if you were to ask me this question as a child, my answer would undoubtedly be strawberry rhubarb pie. Mom had an inventive way of thinking about the future. During spring and summer, she'd freeze pie fillings in advance, ensuring that a homemade pie was just a thaw away. And strawberry rhubarb was always a freezer staple. I can still vividly remember traipsing down to the basement, lifting open the freezer lid, and digging around for that sweet filling. Mom's version was delicious, but baking with rhubarb and strawberries can be a bit tricky. Both fruits have a large amount of water, and as they bake in the oven, they release that liquid, which needs be to thickened to form the filling. The tricky part is finding the right balance, because too much thickener can overshadow the delicate flavors. I found the answer to be simply roasting the fruit. We're accustomed to roasting vegetables or meats, but roasting fruit is almost magical. In the oven, the excess water is cooked off, the sugar intensifies, and the flavors are elevated. The result is a thick, jam-like consistency that's packed with the very essence of the fruit. And the best part is that there's no need for extra thickeners; the natural pectin in the fruit thickens the filling. This pie delivers a flavor punch like no other. Sure, the roasting time is a tad longer, but trust me, it's all hands-off and completely worth every minute!

All-Butter Pie Dough (page 238)

FOR THE FILLING
4 cups quartered hulled strawberries (1½ pounds)
6 cups chopped rhubarb (2 pounds)
¾ cup granulated sugar
2 tablespoons fresh lemon juice

FOR THE CRUMBLE
½ cup all-purpose flour
½ cup packed light brown sugar
¼ cup rolled oats
⅛ teaspoon kosher salt
4 tablespoons unsalted butter, cubed

Make the dough and chill until ready to roll out.

Meanwhile, make the filling: Preheat the oven to 325°F. Line a sheet pan with parchment paper.

In a large bowl, mix together the strawberries, rhubarb, granulated sugar, and lemon juice. Pour onto the lined pan.

Roast until the fruit and liquid are condensed and jam-like, 2 to 2½ hours, stirring as needed if corners get dark. Remove the filling from the oven and set aside. You should have about 2 cups filling.

When ready to bake, preheat the oven to 400°F.

Roll the crust out to a 14-inch round and fit it into a 9-inch pie plate. If uneven, trim the overhang just enough to make the edge around the dish even. Roll under the excess dough to create a crust and crimp. Using a fork, dock the pie shell and refrigerate the crust for 20 minutes.

(recipe continues)

Line the crust with parchment paper and fill with pie weights or dried beans. Bake the crust for 20 minutes. Remove the parchment and weights and reduce the oven temperature to 375°F. Continue baking the crust until it is dried out and beginning to brown, 15 to 20 minutes.

Meanwhile, make the crumble: In a small bowl, combine the flour, brown sugar, rolled oats, and salt. Add the cubed butter and work it into the mixture until it is crumbly.

Once the pie crust is baked, add the prepared filling and smooth to an even layer. Top with the crumble and return the pie to the oven.

Bake the pie until the crumb is golden, 18 to 22 minutes.

Let cool completely before slicing and serving.

Peanut Butter Pie

— Serves 7 to 8 —

I'm not sure if this is a universal experience, but for me at least, when I was growing up, my appreciation for pies went through two distinct phases. First, there was the pudding and custard pie phase—all about that smooth, creamy goodness packed into a pie shell. Anything with fruit or texture, like pecan pies, seemed a bit odd and was reserved only for the grown-ups. Later on, though, something shifted, and I began embracing and maybe even preferring those fruit and specialty seasonal pies. Back in the day, I would only go for pumpkin pie at Thanksgiving, without giving a second thought to pecan. "Why would you want nuts in a pie?" I used to wonder. Pudding pies were my jam, and even though I now enjoy both pecan and pumpkin, my heart still holds a special place for a classic pudding pie. My absolute favorite has to be peanut butter pie. You'd think with a name like that, the filling would be swimming in peanut butter, but the peanut butter pie I adore is a bit different. Some people call it Amish peanut butter pie, and being Mennonite myself, I have to imagine that's probably where it originated. The peanut butter plays a crucial role in the form of crumbles sprinkled on a baked pie shell before being covered by a homemade pudding. And the whipped cream topping is finished off with more of those delightful peanut butter crumbles, which truly are the secret ingredient. And trust me: you have to use the cheap, creamy peanut butter. Do not splurge on fancy artisan peanut butter; it just won't hit the same sweet spot.

All-Butter Pie Dough (page 238)

FOR THE FILLING
1 cup powdered sugar, sifted
¾ cup creamy peanut butter
½ cup heavy cream
2 cups whole milk
4 egg yolks
½ cup granulated sugar
¼ teaspoon kosher salt
¼ cup cornstarch
2 tablespoons unsalted butter
1 teaspoon vanilla extract

FOR THE WHIPPED CREAM TOPPING
1½ cups heavy cream
3 tablespoons powdered sugar, sifted
1 teaspoon vanilla extract
1 tablespoon full-fat Greek yogurt or sour cream

Make and chill the dough as directed. When ready to bake, preheat the oven to 400°F. Roll the crust out to a 14-inch round and fit into a 9-inch pie plate. If uneven, trim the overhang just enough to make the edge around the dish even. Roll under the excess dough to create a crust and crimp. Using a fork, dock the pie shell and refrigerate the crust for 20 minutes.

Line the crust with parchment paper and fill with pie weights or dried beans. Bake the crust for 20 minutes. Remove the parchment and weights and reduce the oven temperature to 375°F.

Continue baking the crust until it is dried out and beginning to brown, 15 to 20 minutes.

(recipe continues)

Make the filling: In a medium bowl, combine the powdered sugar and peanut butter. Using a hand mixer or spoon, mix until the peanut butter and powdered sugar create irregular-sized crumbles. Sprinkle half of the mixture into the baked and cooled pie crust and set both aside.

In a 4-quart saucepan, whisk together the cream, milk, egg yolks, granulated sugar, salt, and cornstarch until smooth. Set the mixture over medium-low heat and whisk constantly until it starts to thicken, 6 to 8 minutes. Continue whisking until the mixture is bubbling throughout and thick, 2 to 4 minutes. Remove from the heat and stir in the butter and vanilla until combined with the pudding. Immediately pour through a sieve into the prepared pie crust with the peanut butter crumbles.

Smooth the top of the pudding and place plastic wrap directly on the pudding so a skin does not form. Refrigerate the pie until the pudding is fully set, 4 to 6 hours.

Make the whipped cream topping: In a large bowl, with an electric mixer, combine the cream, powdered sugar, vanilla, and Greek yogurt. Mix on low until the ingredients are combined and the cream is starting to become foamy. Increase the speed to high and continue to mix until the cream is thick with soft peaks, 4 to 5 minutes.

Spread the whipped topping on top of the chilled pie and top with the remaining peanut butter crumbles.

Breads

Making and baking bread is a lost art. It may be a time-consuming activity, and it takes a bit of experience to understand the feel of dough, but that first whiff of bread in the oven is pure heaven. Don't stress if your first loaf doesn't look utterly perfect; it's all about the incredible taste. Plus, the rhythm of kneading dough and watching the process unfold never gets old. I vividly recall my first attempt at making bread; it wasn't pretty, but knowing that I made it myself made that bread taste so incredibly delicious. And you know what? To this day, I'm just as thrilled every time I start making a new loaf. So, roll up your sleeves, toss some flour on the bench, and lean into these recipes designed to gently guide anyone through the art of baking warm, homemade bread.

Brioche Bread

When I was growing up in my small town, the bread scene was pretty straightforward: wheat, white, and honey oat ruled the field. Brioche and other fancy breads? They weren't exactly readily available in the local supermarket. But if you know me, you know I'm always itching to learn something new, and that extends even to my bread repertoire. Whenever I'd come across something new, like an amazing loaf of brioche bread, you'd better believe that I'd be on a mission to replicate it in my own kitchen. Brioche isn't your run-of-the-mill bread. It's indulgent, with an enriched dough that contains more eggs and butter than other more traditional loaves. And the best part is that working with this dough is super easy. In no time, brioche topped my list of favorite breads for its soft, buttery interior that has tons of flavor, and its deep golden-brown exterior that comes from a luscious egg wash. Nowadays, decades after discovering its magic, I keep a stash of brioche in my freezer, and it truly is my secret weapon for those moments when I want something extra special. Think bread pudding, French toast that's next-level, or even upping the ante with a stellar Thanksgiving stuffing. With this brioche recipe on your side, the possibilities are endless!

5 large eggs
½ cup whole milk, warmed to 100° to 110°F
2 tablespoons neutral oil
½ cup granulated sugar
5 cups all-purpose flour
2¼ teaspoons (1 envelope) instant yeast
1 teaspoon kosher salt
16 tablespoons unsalted butter, at room temperature
Softened butter, for the loaf pans
Egg wash: 1 egg, beaten

In a stand mixer, whisk the eggs, then the warm milk, oil, and sugar. Add the flour and instant yeast. Snap on the dough hook and mix the dough to incorporate the flour and yeast to form a shaggy dough. Add the salt. Knead in the mixer until it pulls away and clears the sides of the bowl, but is slightly tacky, 6 to 8 minutes.

With the mixer on medium-low speed, add the butter 1 tablespoon at a time, allowing the butter to fully incorporate before adding more. Once all of the butter is incorporated, the dough will be smooth and elastic.

Place the dough in an oiled bowl. Cover and allow to rise in a warm area until doubled in size, 1 to 1½ hours.

When the dough is ready, butter two 8½ × 4½-inch loaf pans. Punch the dough down to release the air pockets and separate into 2 equal portions. Knead each portion into a smooth ball and then pat into a 12 × 8-inch rectangle. Roll each rectangle into an 8-inch loaf and place in a prepared loaf pan. Alternatively, the loaves can be braided. Separate each ball of dough into

(recipe continues)

three pieces, roll each piece into 14-inch strands, braid them together, and place the braided dough in a prepared loaf pan, tucking the ends underneath. Cover and set the pans in a warm place to rise until doubled in size, 1 to 1½ hours.

Preheat the oven to 350°F.

When the loaves are ready, brush the top of the loaves with the egg wash. Bake until the bread is deeply golden and registers 190°F on an instant-read thermometer, 35 to 40 minutes.

Let the bread cool in the pan for 5 minutes, then turn out onto a wire rack to cool completely.

Great-Grandma's Sandwich Bread

— Makes 2 loaves —

During the early 1900s, people living in rural areas across the United States became some of the most industrious and well-rounded people. They could do everything, from caring for a farm, fixing and hemming clothes, to putting food on the table three times a day. It wasn't a choice; it was a necessity. In my many conversations with Grandma Conrad, she'd reminisce about the time when presliced bread first became available on grocery store shelves. According to Grandma, even when her mom, Great-Grandma Hirschy, made the move into town, she stuck to making her own butter and bread because store-bought just couldn't compete. Now, I'm not saying this bread recipe is about to make everyone want to abandon the convenience of store-bought loaves forever, but if you ever feel the need to try your hand at baking bread, this foolproof recipe for a classic white loaf is all you need. Each slice is tender and perfect for toast or to use in a sandwich. Personally, I slice up an entire whole loaf and stash it in the freezer. That way, I can pull out a piece whenever the mood strikes, one slice at a time. It's a small nod to the era when making your own bread was the norm, a tradition that we can all continue even today.

2 cups whole milk, warmed to 100° to 110°F
2 tablespoons sugar
4 tablespoons unsalted butter, at room temperature
5 cups bread flour
2¼ teaspoons (1 envelope) instant yeast
2 teaspoons kosher salt
Nonstick baking spray

In a stand mixer (see Note), whisk the milk, sugar, and butter. Whisk until the butter is melted into the milk. Add the bread flour and the instant yeast. Snap on the dough hook and mix on medium-low until a cohesive dough is formed.

Add the salt, turn the mixer to medium speed, and knead the dough until it is smooth and pulls away from the sides of the bowl, clinging to the dough hook, 3 to 4 minutes.

Remove from the mixer and knead on a floured surface to form a smooth ball. Place the dough in a lightly oiled bowl. Cover and set in a warm place to rise until doubled in size, 1 to 1½ hours.

When the dough has doubled in size, grease two 8½ × 4½-inch standard or 9 × 4-inch Pullman loaf pans.

Punch the dough to release any air bubbles. Separate the dough into 2 equal portions and knead into balls. Pat each ball into a 12 × 8-inch rectangle. Roll up into an 8-inch loaf and place each one in a prepared loaf pan. Cover and set in a warm place until they are doubled in size, 45 minutes to 1 hour. *(recipe continues)*

Position a rack in the lower third of the oven and preheat the oven to 350°F.

Bake the bread until the tops are golden and the bread registers 190° to 200°F on an instant-read thermometer, 20 to 25 minutes.

Let the bread cool in the pans for 5 minutes, then turn out onto a wire rack to cool completely.

Note: A large bowl and Danish or dough whisk can be used in place of a stand mixer.

Cinnamon Swirl Pumpkin Bread

— Makes 2 loaves —

Homemade bread is like a warm, doughy hug, and there's something about the act of making, or even receiving, a freshly baked batch that just makes you happy. Not to mention, the house will smell amazing. This bread combines two of my favorite things: pumpkin and cinnamon toast. Mom used to whip up some cinnamon sugar toast whenever my sister or I felt a bit off. It was like a warm, snug blanket in food form, perfect for those "I don't know if I'm that sick, but maybe I should skip school today" mornings. After a slice of that toast, we'd hop on the bus, our taste buds ready for the day. You might be wondering about the pumpkin twist and why I added it if Mom's version was so perfect. Pumpkin not only screams fall, but it also brings a moist texture to the bread due to the pumpkin's level of water content. So, if you're aiming for the ultimate toast, French toast, or just a delicious treat, this is your go-to recipe. Homemade bread just tastes different, especially when it's filled with the goodness of pumpkin and cinnamon.

¼ cup whole milk
3 tablespoons unsalted butter
⅓ cup maple syrup
One 15-ounce can pumpkin puree
5½ cups all-purpose flour
2¼ teaspoons (1 envelope) instant yeast
1 tablespoon kosher salt
¼ cup sugar
2 tablespoons ground cinnamon
Nonstick baking spray

In a small saucepan, heat the milk and butter together until the butter is melted and pour the mixture into the bowl of a stand mixer. Stir in the maple syrup and pumpkin puree.

Snap on the dough hook, add the flour and instant yeast, and mix until incorporated. Add the salt and continue to mix on medium speed until the dough pulls away from the sides of the bowl, 4 to 6 minutes.

Remove the dough from the bowl and knead on a lightly floured surface until it is smooth, 3 to 4 minutes. Place in a lightly oiled bowl, cover, and set it in a warm spot until doubled in size, 1 to 1½ hours.

In a small bowl, combine the sugar and cinnamon. Mix evenly and set it aside.

Grease two 8½ × 4½-inch loaf pans.

Once the dough has risen, punch it down and knead it into a smooth ball. Divide the dough into 2 equal portions. Working with one half at a time, press the dough out into a 12 × 8-inch rectangle. Spread half of the cinnamon sugar over the dough. With a short side of the rectangle facing you, roll the dough up into a log. Lay the log

(recipe continues)

in one of the prepared loaf pans with the seam side down. Repeat with the remaining portion of dough and cinnamon sugar. Cover the loaves and set them in a warm spot to rise until they reach the top of the pans, about 45 minutes.

Preheat the oven to 350°F.

Bake the bread until it is golden brown and the internal temperature reaches 195° to 200°F, 30 to 40 minutes.

Let the breads cool in the pans for 20 minutes, then turn out onto a wire rack to cool completely.

Swedish Limpa Bread

— Makes 2 loaves —

One day, while working in the kitchen with Grandma Conrad and Mom, the conversation naturally gravitated toward bread. More likely than not, I was bombarding them with questions about their favorite breads and the ones they used to make. That's when they looked at each other, and both voiced their love for Great-Grandma's Swedish limpa bread. My immediate response was to ask them why they weren't making it themselves. To my surprise, both admitted that their attempts always ended in a disappointing dense and dry loaf. If you're not acquainted with limpa, it's a classic rye bread known for its soft and tender crumb. The secret weapon is buttermilk, which works to tenderize the rye flour, yielding the perfect loaf. Since I knew they both loved this bread, I took it upon myself to remedy the situation. I've found that the key lies in the ratio of rye to all-purpose flour. Rye flour, with its lower gluten content compared to traditional white flour, can be a bit finicky to use. By using the correct balance of rye and all-purpose flour, Great-Grandma's bread recipe is reborn. This bread is a true multitasker, as it's perfect for a quick smoked salmon appetizer or as the foundation of your favorite sandwich. It's the kind of bread that brings a touch of tradition to the table while easily adapting to whatever dish you have in mind.

2 cups buttermilk, warmed to 100°F
2 tablespoons unsalted butter
2 tablespoons sugar
¼ cup molasses
2 cups dark rye flour
3 cups all-purpose flour
¼ teaspoon baking soda
¼ teaspoon baking powder
2¼ teaspoons (1 envelope) instant yeast
2 teaspoons kosher salt
Softened butter, for the loaf pans

In a stand mixer fitted with the dough hook, combine the buttermilk, butter, sugar, molasses, rye flour, all-purpose flour, baking soda, baking powder, and instant yeast. Mix on low to combine. Add the salt and mix on medium until the dough is smooth and pulling away from the sides of the bowl, 4 to 6 minutes.

Remove the dough from the bowl and knead by hand into a smooth ball. Place the dough in a lightly oiled bowl. Cover, set in a warm place, and allow the dough to rise until doubled in size, 1½ to 2 hours.

Butter two 8½ × 4½-inch loaf pans and set aside.

Once risen, punch down the dough, remove it from the bowl, and divide it into 2 equal portions. Knead each half of the dough into a smooth oval and place into a prepared loaf pan. Cover the bread, set it in a warm place, and let rise until the dough is about doubled in size, 45 minutes to 1 hour.

Preheat the oven to 350°F. *(recipe continues)*

Bake until the bread is deep brown and registers 190°F on an instant-read thermometer, 28 to 32 minutes.

Let the bread cool in the pans for 5 minutes, then turn out onto a wire rack to cool completely.

Mom's No-Knead Failproof Bread

— Makes 1 loaf —

I go through these phases where I'm all for baking my own bread, and then I sort of fall out of the routine and end up buying loaves from the store for months. The real challenge is getting back into the swing of bread baking, and if you're new to bread making, it can seem a bit daunting to figure out where to begin. Well, this is the go-to recipe, whether you're a first-time bread baker or excited to rekindle your love for bread making. My mom used to call this recipe "cottage bread," because you can switch out the buttermilk for blended cottage cheese. We always had cottage cheese around, and those summer lunches with a cold-cut sandwich and a side of cottage cheese still hold a special place in my memory. Cottage cheese works great, but if you really want to take the flavor up a notch, make sure to use buttermilk. The real beauty of this bread, though, lies in its simplicity, making it taste like you've put in way more effort than you actually have. It's a wet, shaggy dough that comes together in no time, so forget about any kneading. It rises and bakes in an ovenproof glass bowl, giving you that classic boule shape. Say hello to homemade bread that's simple enough to keep you from falling off the bread-baking wagon.

1 cup buttermilk
2 tablespoons honey
2 tablespoons unsalted butter, melted
1 large egg, beaten
1¾ cups all-purpose flour
½ cup whole wheat flour
2 tablespoons wheat germ
1 teaspoon kosher salt
2¼ teaspoons (1 envelope) instant yeast
¼ teaspoon baking soda
Nonstick baking spray

In a large bowl, combine the buttermilk, honey, melted butter, and egg. Whisk until smooth. Add the all-purpose flour, whole wheat flour, wheat germ, salt, yeast, and baking soda. Using a fork or Danish (dough) whisk, combine the ingredients into a wet, shaggy dough. Mix until the dough just begins to clear the sides of the bowl. Drizzle a bowl with neutral oil and roll the dough in the oil. Cover and allow the dough to rise for 1 hour. Do not worry about making sure the dough is doubled in size.

Punch the dough down and form it into a ball. Place the ball in a greased 4-quart ovenproof bowl. Let the dough rise for an additional 40 minutes.

Meanwhile, preheat the oven to 350°F.

Bake until the bread is golden with an internal temperature of 190°F, 40 to 50 minutes.

Let the bread cool in the bowl for 5 minutes, then turn out onto a wire rack to cool completely.

Herb & Cheese Butterhorns

— Makes 24 rolls —

Butterhorns are the great equalizer at any dinner table. You might have a picky eater glaring at the main dish, and others turning up their noses at the salad, but rest assured, everyone's reaching for the butterhorns. I'm convinced these were the home baker's easier-to-make response to the challenge of preparing croissants. I imagine that at one point in time, someone had a perfect croissant, got inspired to re-create them at home, only to realize that croissants are a serious labor of love. Enter butterhorns, the melt-in-your-mouth alternative born of practicality. Just talking about them is making me salivate! Sure, butterhorns take some time to prepare, but nothing compared to the effort necessary for croissants. The dough is easy, enriched with butter, and before being rolled up, they get a sprinkle of herbs and cheese for that extra savory filling. Fair warning: when making these, it's mandatory to sample several straight from the oven—you know, strictly for quality assurance purposes.

FOR THE DOUGH
- 5 tablespoons unsalted butter, at room temperature
- 1/3 cup sugar
- 1 teaspoon kosher salt
- 2/3 cup whole milk, warmed to 110°F
- 2 large eggs, beaten
- 3½ cups all-purpose flour
- 2¼ teaspoons (1 envelope) instant yeast

FOR THE HERB & CHEESE FILLING
- 5 tablespoons unsalted butter, plus 2 tablespoons butter, melted, for brushing
- ½ teaspoon garlic powder
- ¼ teaspoon onion powder
- 1 teaspoon minced fresh thyme
- 1 teaspoon minced fresh rosemary
- ¼ teaspoon kosher salt
- 1 cup grated pecorino cheese

Make the dough: In a stand mixer fitted with the dough hook, combine the butter, sugar, and salt. Pour the warmed milk into the bowl. Mix until the butter and sugar are dissolved.

Mix in the beaten eggs. Add the flour and yeast. Use the stand mixer (or by hand) to knead the dough until it is smooth and beginning to pull away from the sides of the bowl, 6 to 8 minutes.

Once the dough clears the side of the mixer bowl and is slightly tacky, remove the dough and knead a few times by hand on a lightly floured surface. The dough should be slightly tacky but not stick to the board while continually kneading.

Put the dough in a large oiled bowl, cover with a damp towel (or plastic wrap), and set in a warm place to rise until doubled, 1 to 1½ hours.

(recipe continues)

When the dough is ready, make the filling: In a small saucepan, combine 5 tablespoons of the butter, the garlic powder, onion powder, thyme, rosemary, and salt. Melt over low heat. Remove the herb butter from the heat.

Punch down the dough and divide it into 2 equal portions. Shape each half into a ball and punch out any air bubbles. On a well-floured surface, roll out each dough ball to a 14-inch round about ¼ inch thick. Brush each round with the herb butter and sprinkle with the pecorino.

Line two baking sheets with parchment paper. Cut into each round into 12 wedges, as one would for a pizza. Start by cutting in quarters, then each quarter into 3 triangles. Take one triangle, stretch the wide end slightly, and starting from the wide end, roll up tightly toward the point. Pinch the ends to create a seal, then place the butterhorn seam side down on the lined baking sheets. Let the butterhorns rise until they are about doubled in size, 45 minutes.

Meanwhile, position racks in the top and bottom thirds of the oven and preheat to 350°F.

Bake until the rolls are lightly golden on top, 10 to 15 minutes, switching racks halfway through baking and watching carefully to ensure the tops and bottoms do not overbake but turn lightly golden.

Remove from the oven and brush with the melted butter. Let cool, but serve warm.

Thank You . . .

To all the Wyse Guide followers and cheerleaders who continue to show kindness and excitement for the passions in my life. When Wyse Guide began in 2012, I was a small-town Iowa farm kid with no idea what I was doing. But your kindness and excitement showed me that my Iowa life was far from boring. You rallied around my projects, outdoors and in the kitchen, in ways I never could have expected. Nothing will ever compare to the joy I feel when I see my recipes included in your gatherings and weeknight meals.

To Joel Kratzer for cocreating Wyse Guide and taking on the role of photographer and food stylist for this book. It's rare that two people work together in a way where one picks up what the other lacks. Wyse Guide is only possible with your work behind the scenes and your constant creative vision for all things design. Because of you, my words sound better, my food looks more tasty, and my projects are captured flawlessly.

To my mom, because without you, I would have no words on the pages, no stories to tell, and no amazing childhood. Thank you for always allowing me to create. From painting mint leaves with chocolate when I was eight years old because I saw it on TV to putting in my first flower bed that I designed on my own, you have always given me the freedom to express myself in any way I choose.

To my sister, Kelsey, for testing many of the recipes in the book. You will always be my biggest cheerleader and first follower who knew Wyse Guide could happen, even before me.

To McCade, who edits all my videos and assisted with the photography in this book. You were thrown into this process right in the middle and helped willingly and without question.

To Deb, Emma, Melissa, and the entire Harvest team, thank you for believing I had a voice and a story worth telling through the food I make. Thank you for putting up with all my questions, worries, and design details. You've made this book truly feel like me.

To Sheraton, Gary, Megan, and Rachel, you are all more than I could ask for in a friend. You have believed I can do things I never thought I would and continue to believe in me even when I don't see it. Thank you for being who you are and part of my life.

Universal Conversion Chart

Oven temperature equivalents

250°F = 120°C	275°F = 135°C	300°F = 150°C	325°F = 160°C
350°F = 180°C	375°F = 190°C	400°F = 200°C	425°F = 220°C
450°F = 230°C	475°F = 240°C	500°F = 260°C	

Measurement equivalents

Measurements should always be level unless directed otherwise.

⅛ teaspoon = 0.5 mL	¼ teaspoon = 1 mL	½ teaspoon = 2 mL	1 teaspoon = 5 mL
1 tablespoon = 3 teaspoons = ½ fluid ounce = 15 mL	2 tablespoons = ⅛ cup = 1 fluid ounce = 30 mL	4 tablespoons = ¼ cup = 2 fluid ounces = 60 mL	5⅓ tablespoons = ⅓ cup = 3 fluid ounces = 80 mL
8 tablespoons = ½ cup = 4 fluid ounces = 120 mL	10⅔ tablespoons = ⅔ cup = 5 fluid ounces = 160 mL	12 tablespoons = ¾ cup = 6 fluid ounces = 180 mL	16 tablespoons = 1 cup = 8 fluid ounces = 240 mL

Index

Note: Page references in *italics* refer to photos of recipes and recipe preparation.

HarperCollins books may be purchased for
educational, business, or sales promotional use.
For information, please email the Special Markets
Department at SPsales@harpercollins.com.

FIRST EDITION

Designed by Melissa Lotfy
Photography by Joel Kratzer

Library of Congress Cataloging-in-Publication
Data has been applied for.

ISBN 978-0-06-334571-3

25 26 27 28 29 cos 10 9 8 7 6 5 4 3 2 1